EASTERN FRONT FROM PRIMARY SOURCES

EASTERN FRONT
ENCIRCLEMENT AND ESCAPE BY GERMAN FORCES

Centre of Military History
United States Army, Washington, D.C.

INTRODUCED BY

BOB CARRUTHERS

Pen & Sword
MILITARY

This edition published in 2013 by
Pen & Sword Military
An imprint of
Pen & Sword Books Ltd
47 Church Street
Barnsley
South Yorkshire
S70 2AS

First published in Great Britain in 2011 in digital format by
Coda Books Ltd.

Copyright © Coda Books Ltd, 2011
Published under licence by Pen & Sword Books Ltd.

ISBN 978 1 78159 221 2

A CIP catalogue record for this book is
available from the British Library

Printed and bound by CPI Group (UK) Ltd, Croydon, CR0 4YY

Pen & Sword Books Ltd incorporates the Imprints of Pen & Sword Aviation, Pen &
Sword Family History, Pen & Sword Maritime, Pen & Sword Military, Pen &
Sword Discovery, Pen & Sword Politics, Pen & Sword Atlas, Pen & Sword
Archaeology, Wharncliffe Local History, Wharncliffe True Crime, Wharncliffe
Transport, Pen & Sword Select, Pen & Sword Military Classics, Leo Cooper, The
Praetorian Press, Claymore Press, Remember When, Seaforth Publishing and
Frontline Publishing

For a complete list of Pen & Sword titles please contact
PEN & SWORD BOOKS LIMITED
47 Church Street, Barnsley, South Yorkshire, S70 2AS, England
E-mail: enquiries@pen-and-sword.co.uk
Website: www.pen-and-sword.co.uk

CONTENTS

INTRODUCTION

THE HISTORICAL record demonstrates that Adolf Hitler was a gambler who, throughout his notorious career, took a series of calculated risks. Initially these marginal ventures were carefully considered, and Hitler emerged the winner from his high stake bets that Britain and France would remain supine in the face of Hitler's actions in the Rhineland, Sudetenland, Czechoslovakia and Austria. Inevitably Hitler drew the wrong conclusions from his early run of luck and began to make the series of mistakes which were to lead to the outbreak of World War II and his own destruction. The decision to invade Soviet Russia unleashed Hitler's personal nemesis in the form of the Red Army, however, it is arguable that Hitler's biggest mistake of all was to drag a reluctant US into World War II. Even after the Japanese attack on Pearl Harbour Hitler still had the option to keep the US out of the war. In a typical act of self -delusion Hitler, on 11th December 1941, declared war on the largest industrial nation on earth. From that moment onwards the fate of Nazi Germany was sealed. It took some months to awake the sleeping giant, but once the US Juggernaut began to roll the end result of World War II was never in question.

While the US was busy assembling its new armies, navies and air forces, the US Intelligence Service was already beginning to collate intelligence on its new enemy. This information was assembled and disseminated to the troops who needed it, in the form of two main monthly intelligence bulletins. These were *Tactical and Technical Trends* which first appeared in June 1942 and the *Intelligence Bulletin* which began to appear from September 1942 onwards.

The main focus for the US was initially on the war with Japan and a great majority of the early reports are concerned with the war in the Pacific. However, as America began to come up to speed US forces were soon engaged in North Africa followed by Sicily, Italy and finally Northern Europe. As the war progressed the requirement for good intelligence of German battlefield tactics

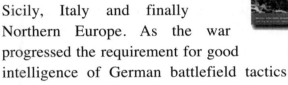

became more and more important and in consequence there are more and more reports of German fighting techniques available to us. The vast majority of those reports concerned the fighting in Russia and it is those reports which form the bulk of what you are about to read here.

After the war it soon became apparent that the cold war was already underway and the nature of US intelligence reports quickly changed from a grudgingly pro-soviet stance to guarded watchfulness. The 1946 pieces which are reproduced here were written with a view to facing the Soviets as enemies rather than allies.

The material for the two US intelligence journals was originally collected from British combat reports, German newspapers, captured German documents, German training manuals and various Soviet sources. As such, the quality of much of what was printed was highly variable, some reports are highly accurate while, in others, the precision of the information is questionable to say the least, but that's what makes these reports so fascinating. Regardless of the overall accuracy, this is a priceless glimpse into how the men in the front lines learned about their enemy, and as such it presents us with a invaluable insight into the events of the Eastern Front were perceived at the time when they actually unfolded. The reports also provide us with a host of information concerning the minor aspects of the thousands of tactical combats being waged day in and day out which expand our knowledge of the realities of the fighting in Russia.

Following the final collapse and unconditional surrender of the Wehrmacht in May 1945 the long hoped for peace in Europe had finally arrived. Unfortunately the tensions, which soon developed into the cold war, appeared almost immediately. As relations between the former allies cooled the prospect of an armed clash loomed on the horizon Britain and America had to face up to the possibility that they could soon find themselves lining up alongside the men of the recently defeated Wehrmacht in a fight to the death with Red Army.

With that appalling prospect in mind the pool of hard won knowledge which existed in the upper echelons of the Wehrmacht was invaluable and had to be collected and systematically recycled to the US and British forces as quickly and as thoroughly as possible.

Senior Luftwaffe figures such as Adolf Galland were to prove extremely valuable in delivering the crucial experience of the war in the air. The material for this and other studies of World War II on land was prepared by a group of former German generals and general staff officers including Erhrad Rauss. The extensive interview programme eventually appeared as the German Report Series and today they represent a fascinating glimpse from the operational and tactical viewpoint of the war in the east at the sharp end.

Germans who had witnessed the events at first hand wrote these unique publications. They are told exclusively from the German point of view. The principal author was former Brig. Gen. Alfred Toppe, he and most of his associates served for extended periods on the Russian Front during World War II. Most of the group could boast combined experience of combat and staff work. Crucially most of them held assignments involving troop training, which would prove invaluable in the event that US or British forces might have to cross swords with the Soviets.

There is therefore a strong emphasis on not just absorbing the lessons but also on training which runs as a theme throughout the German Report series. The writers were only too aware that had events taken the wrong turn the next stage in this process might have been the preparation of actual training manuals for GIs on their way to a second Russian Front.

The US Foreign Studies Branch, Special Studies Division, and Office of the Chief of Military History carried out the original editing of this study. The draft translation of each the original German texts was first revised and then reorganized in the interest of brevity, clarity, and pertinence. In this process every effort was made by the original editors to retain the point of view, the expressions, and even the prejudices of the German authors. To modern readers some of the sentiments may appear unreconstructed and extremely hostile, as such they are clearly "of their time " but they do represent a real wealth of detail on the war in the east from an original point of view, with the passing time the sources those sources are now lost to us.

As historians, students of history or general readers we should all be grateful for the work which was undertaken by these former enemies during the 40's and 50's which now affords an extensive inside record of an experience from highly trustworthy sources concerning the terrible events which all of us can be thankful that we did not have to share.

Thank you for buying this book. I hope you enjoy reading these long forgotten reports as much as I enjoyed discovering them and collating them for you. Other volumes in this series are already in preparation and I hope you will decide to join me in other discoveries as the series develops.

Bob Carruthers

PREFACE:
OPERATIONS OF ENCIRCLED
FORCES - GERMAN
EXPERIENCES IN RUSSIA

THIS PAMPHLET was prepared by a committee of former German officers under the supervision of the Historical Division, EUCOM. Among the contributors were former corps commanders and general staff officers at corps, army, and army group level, who had extensive experience on the Russian front during the period 1941-45. The main author, for instance, saw action before Leningrad, near Voronezh, and later at Stalingrad. Toward the end of the war he served successively as chief of staff of Army Groups North and Center, during their withdrawal from Russia.

In addition to discussing the tactical and logistical problems peculiar to operations of encircled forces, the authors take issue with Hitler's conviction that significant advantages can be gained by leaving isolated forces behind the advancing enemy lines. It was this notion, expressed in numerous specific orders, that made the desperate stand of encircled German troops a frequent occurrence during the Russian campaign.

The problems of air support for encircled ground troops are described in a separate appendix which deals with tactical air support, air reconnaissance, supply by air, and the employment of antiaircraft units. Based on the experiences of the German Air Force in Russia and presented by a former Luftwaffe officer, the views expressed are necessarily colored by the organizational peculiarities of the Luftwaffe and its relations to the German

Army.

The reader is reminded that publications in the GERMAN REPORT SERIES were written by Germans from the German point of view and are presented without interpretation by American personnel. Minor changes in form and in chapter headings have been made to secure greater clarity. However, passages which reflect the authors' prejudices and defects, whatever they may be, have not been changed and find the same expression in the following translation as they do in the original German.

This pamphlet supersedes MS T-12, "Operations of Encircled Forces," which was given a limited distribution by the Office of the Chief of Military History, Special Staff, U.S. Army.

CHAPTER I: ENCIRCLED FORCES
INTRODUCTION

POCKETS ARE formed as the result of operations in which the attacker entirely surrounds a large number of the opposing forces. Such encirclement is usually followed by a battle of annihilation, the classic goal of all types of ground combat. The principles involved in carrying out penetrations and envelopments, and in closing the ring around an enemy force are well established in tactical doctrine. In the following study, however, the problem is approached exclusively from the defender's point of view. German pockets in Russia - often the result of peremptory orders to hold out in the face of certain encirclement - are used as examples to illustrate the tactical principles applied by the encircled units and the measures taken in each instance to permit a breakout in the direction of the German lines.

The experiences of World War II demonstrate that under conditions of modern, mobile warfare such pockets are more easily created than in military operations of the past. Their tactical significance has changed considerably. The encirclement of military forces by the enemy no longer signals the end of their usefulness. Pockets have become frequent occurrences in modern combat and must be countered by appropriate tactical measures designed to tie down large numbers of the enemy and, eventually, to rescue the encircled troops.

Generally, encirclements are effected by an opponent with considerable superiority in men and materiel. Without these prerequisites, only superior planning can lead to the entrapment of substantial military forces. Such cases are extremely rare.

The maneuver of deliberately allowing one's forces to be

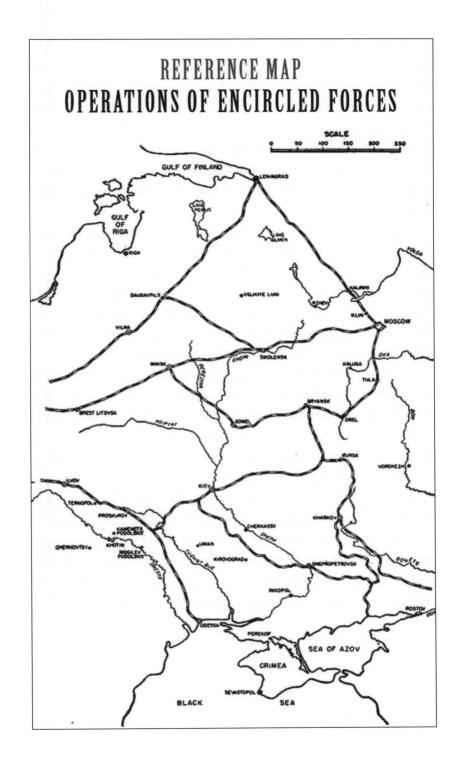

REFERENCE MAP
OPERATIONS OF ENCIRCLED FORCES

encircled by the enemy so as to tie up his troops in sufficient numbers to even the odds, rarely achieves the desired result. Should the total opposing forces be approximately equal, such a maneuver can be of value, but only if the number of enemy troops engaged in maintaining the encirclement is large enough to affect the outcome of other operations. Even in this case, however, the deliberate creation of a pocket is a costly enterprise which will hardly justify the probable loss of the entire encircled force.

Success or failure of the encircled troops in fighting their way back to the German lines depended almost entirely on the tactical situation in and around the pocket. Whereas a discussion of strategic decisions is normally outside the scope of tactical studies, the situations described in the following chapters are the direct result of decisions by higher headquarters and can only be understood against the background of these decisions.

In addition to minor German pockets in Russia, the battles of encirclement near Cherkassy and Kamenets-Podolskiy (Chapters 4 and 5) have been selected as typical examples of large-scale pocket engagements and breakout attempts. In Chapter 4, furthermore, the report on developments inside the pocket is contrasted with impressions gained of the same operation by an officer at a higher headquarters outside the ring of encirclement. Excerpts from the diary of a German pocket commander show the increasing psychological pressure exerted by the enemy on encircled troops, especially the attempt at persuasion by the so-called Committee for a Free Germany, which was organized by the Russians and composed of captured German officers.

THE POCKET OF KLIN - BREAKOUT OF A PANZER DIVISION

W HEN THE German offensive against Moscow came to a halt on 6 December 1941, the 1st Panzer Division was located at a point fifteen miles north of the Russian capital. It was immediately ordered back to Klin (Map 1) with the mission of keeping that town open for the withdrawal of other German armored forces. Deep snow obstructed every movement, and the highway running through Klin was the only route over which the withdrawal of mechanized and motorized columns could be effected.

The division reached Klin, after fighting the elements as well as the enemy, and succeeded in holding that important junction against persistent Russian attacks until the retrograde movements of other German units through the town were completed. At that point, however, as the division was ready to break contact and withdraw in the direction of Nekrasino, it found itself completely surrounded by strong enemy forces. The division was ordered by higher headquarters to abandon its vehicles if necessary, and to break through to Nekrasino where it would be able to link up with other German forces.

During the days of heavy fighting that preceded the entry of the division into Klin, the road to Nekrasino had been cut by the enemy on several occasions. In these engagements other German units lost numerous vehicles by enemy action and collisions. Wrecks had piled up all along the road and left no more than a narrow lane between them.

By reconnaissance in force, the encircled division discovered

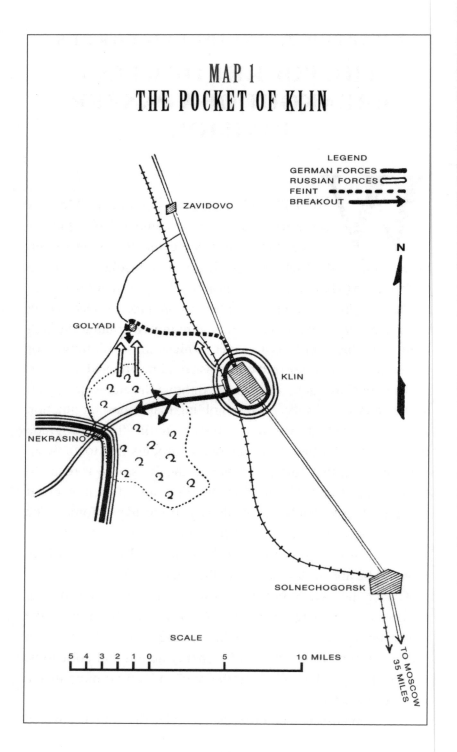

MAP 1
THE POCKET OF KLIN

LEGEND
GERMAN FORCES
RUSSIAN FORCES
FEINT
BREAKOUT

N

ZAVIDOVO

GOLYADI

KLIN

NEKRASINO

SOLNECHOGORSK

TO MOSCOW
35 MILES

SCALE

5 4 3 2 1 0   5   10 MILES

that enemy resistance was weakest southeast of Klin, and that a breakout in this direction would be most likely to succeed. The terrain, however, was such that practically all vehicles would have to be left behind. There were from 800 to 1,000 wounded in Klin who could not be evacuated without transportation. Furthermore, despite considerable loss of equipment, the encircled force was still well provided with vehicles and not inclined to give them up, if that could possibly be avoided.

After short deliberation it was agreed that the division, in order to retain its mobility, would have to break out along the road to Nekra-sino, although that road itself was held by enemy forces in considerable strength. Chiefly responsible for this decision was the large number of casualties that were to be evacuated at any cost.

In preparing for the breakout, the division made use of its experiences during a previous encirclement at Kalinin. There, after executing a feint in a different direction which diverted some of the hostile forces, the division had succeeded in making a surprise breakout, losing no equipment and suffering few casualties. The great flexibility of the artillery had been of decisive importance. Shifting their fire rapidly from one target to the other, all pieces were able to support the diversionary attack as well as the actual breakout. Equally important had been the possibility of throwing all the tanks that survived the diversionary maneuver into the main effort.

After a careful survey of the situation around Klin, a plan was adopted. All available tanks, one company of armored infantry and one rifle battalion were to conduct a diversionary break-through north of Klin, and then to proceed in a westerly direction toward the town of Golyadi. Turning sharply south after reaching Golyadi, these forces were to initiate an attack in the direction of the main road. The artillery was to remain in position around the railroad station of Klin. The main breakout toward Nekrasino was to take place as soon as the Russians reacted to the threat near Golyadi and began to divert their forces from the main road.

The Germans calculated that the turning movement at Golyadi would force the enemy to shift his front toward the north in order to avoid envelopment from that direction. Initially, the entire German artillery and all available antiaircraft weapons were to support the forces carrying out the feint.

While all remained quiet in the area designated for the main effort, the German units were assembled in proper order inside the encircled city. H Hour for the diversionary maneuver - actually an attack with limited objective - was set for dawn. The time of the main break-through depended on the development of the situation.

The intended deception of the enemy was accomplished with full success. A well-organized German task force fell upon the Russians at Golyadi and caught them by surprise. At the appearance of German tanks the Russians immediately shifted their reserves to meet the diversionary attack which they assumed to be the main German breakout. The attacking German troops, incidentally, had not been informed that their effort at Golyadi was no more than a feint. It was felt that they would not fight with quite the same zeal if they knew that they were merely trying to deceive the enemy. Only the division artillery commander was entrusted with the full details of the plan, including the code word for shifting fire to his new targets on either side of the Klin-Nekrasino road. The German task force took Golyadi and pivoted south. As expected, the enemy began to pull out from the area of the main road and to move north across the railroad line, determined to counter the threat of envelopment.

This was the appropriate time - about noon of the same day - to launch the main breakout along the road to Nekrasino. Upon prearranged signal, artillery and antiaircraft weapons shifted their fire. Only one artillery battalion continued to fire on the old target so as to cover the withdrawal of the diversionary force from Golyadi. Simultaneously, on the road leading out of Klin toward the west, the main attack got under way. The division's armored infantry battalion drove the first gap into the lines of an enemy taken completely by surprise. Dismounted armored infantry and motorcycle troops followed and widened the penetration. Some of the tanks initially engaged in the diversionary maneuver had made their way back to Klin and were now committed on both sides of the road. Under their protection, the wounded on trucks and sleds and accompanied by armored personnel carriers were moved out of the town. By now the artillery was covering the flanks of the break-through column. In the eastern part of the city combat engineers held off the enemy while the evacuation took its course. With the rate of progress determined by the movement of numerous vehicles, and by the need for gradual displacement of the artillery which was in turn covered by tanks and armored cars operating north and south of the road, the entire force fought its way through to Nekrasino, where it was received by other German units.

Undoubtedly the division owed much of its success to the proper employment of its combat elements, but it was primarily the maintenance of strict traffic control that permitted the evacuation of an unusually large number of vehicles and thus determined the outcome of the entire operation. All vehicles that broke down were immediately pushed off the road to keep the column moving without interruption. A large number of officers and noncommissioned officers with minor combat injuries had been added to the military police to assist in the strict enforcement of traffic discipline. The division staff, at first located at the western edge of Klin and later with the main body of the division, directed the initial break-through and the subsequent movements of individual elements with the use of radio and messengers, but without telephone communications.

Substantially intact, the division emerged from the pocket of Klin, taking along its casualties and nearly all of its equipment. Twenty-four hours later, on a different sector of the front, it was again in action against the enemy.

ENCIRCLEMENT AT VELIKIYE LUKI - FAILURE OF A RESCUE OPERATION

BY MID-NOVEMBER 1942 the northernmost corps sector of Army Group Center extended seventy miles, from the town of Velizh north to the army group boundary. Inadequately covered by LIX Corps, the line contained two large gaps, each about ten miles wide and partly swampy but not entirely impassable. There, only reconnaissance and combat patrols provided a minimum of security. Despite persistent requests by the army group commander, no reinforcements arrived to strengthen the precarious German defenses on that sector.

Late in November the Russians attacked north and south of Velikiye Luki (Map 2) and succeeded in encircling the city which was held by a strong regimental combat team of the 83d Division. A few miles farther south two additional German combat teams suffered the same fate. Thus three separate German pockets completely cut off from the main force were created in the same general area.

By that time all available reserves of Army Group Center had been thrown into the fierce battle at Rzhev and could not be extricated for the relief of the encircled units in the Velikiye Luki area. The army group commander therefore requested authority from Army High Command to order breakouts of the encircled forces toward the west. If carried out at once, these could have been accomplished without great difficulty or excessive casualties, but it would have meant pulling the German line back

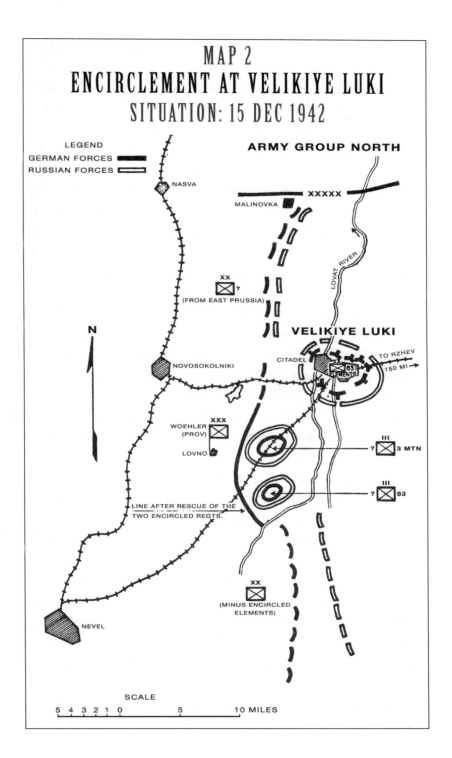

MAP 2
ENCIRCLEMENT AT VELIKIYE LUKI
SITUATION: 15 DEC 1942

LEGEND
GERMAN FORCES
RUSSIAN FORCES

ARMY GROUP NORTH

NASVA

MALINOVKA

XXXXX

LOVAT RIVER

XX
?
(FROM EAST PRUSSIA)

N

VELIKIYE LUKI

NOVOSOKOLNIKI

CITADEL

63
ELEMENTS

TO RZHEV
150 MI

XXX
WOEHLER
(PROV)

LOVNO

III
? 3 MTN

III
? 63

LINE AFTER RESCUE OF THE
TWO ENCIRCLED REGTS.

XX
(MINUS ENCIRCLED
ELEMENTS)

NEVEL

SCALE
5 4 3 2 1 0   5   10 MILES

about ten to fifteen miles. The new defense positions, as proposed by army group, would still assure the undisturbed operation of the Nevel-Novosokolniki-Nasva railroad, and the resulting Russian salient was then to be reduced, as soon as possible, by a German flank attack from the south.

Hitler, who in December 1941 had assumed direct control of all military operations in Russia, flatly rejected this proposal. Instead, he ordered that the pockets be held at all costs, that other German forces, by attacking from the west, re-establish contact with the encircled units, and that the front be pushed even farther to the east. He referred to a recent German success in a similar situation at Kholm by the same officer who now commanded the 83d Division in the area of Velikiye Luki. Army group tried in vain to call Hitler's attention to the lack of reserves and the extreme hardships imposed by winter weather and difficult terrain. All such representations were impatiently brushed aside.

The two German combat teams surrounded in the area south of Velikiye Luki meanwhile conducted a fighting withdrawal toward the west. With the assistance of other German forces, they broke out of encirclement and succeeded in establishing a new front.

At Velikiye Luki the Germans had previously constructed a perimeter of hasty field fortifications around the town. Advance positions, located several hundred yards from the edge of the city, proved of considerable value during the initial stages of the siege. The encircled garrison consisted of a strong infantry regiment of the 83d Division, two artillery battalions, one observation battalion, one engineer company, two construction battalions, and strong service and supply units. The pocket commander, a lieutenant colonel, had assumed command of his regiment only a few days earlier, and accordingly did not know his troops.

The enemy had so disposed his forces that at the beginning of December only two Russian brigades were deployed in a wide

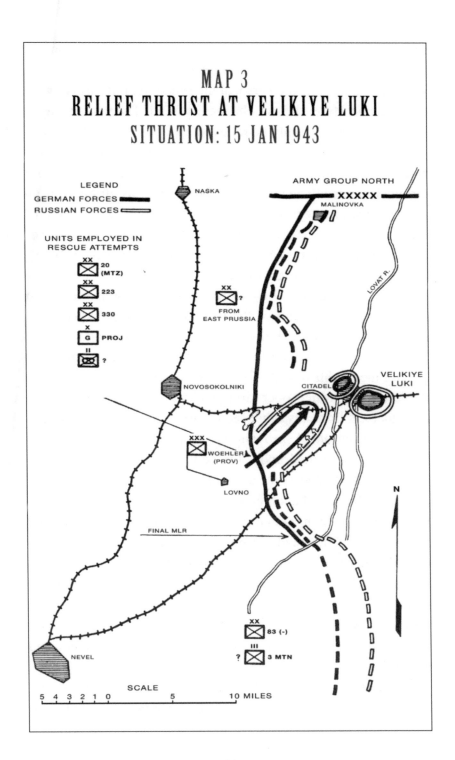

MAP 3
RELIEF THRUST AT VELIKIYE LUKI
SITUATION: 15 JAN 1943

LEGEND
GERMAN FORCES
RUSSIAN FORCES

UNITS EMPLOYED IN
RESCUE ATTEMPTS

20 (MTZ)

223

330

G PROJ

?

NASKA

ARMY GROUP NORTH

XXXXX

MALINOVKA

LOVAT R.

FROM
EAST PRUSSIA

NOVOSOKOLNIKI

CITADEL

VELIKIYE
LUKI

WOEHLER
(PROV)

LOVNO

N

FINAL MLR

83 (-)

? 3 MTN

NEVEL

SCALE
5 4 3 2 1 0   5   10 MILES

arc west of Velikiye Luki. As late as two weeks after the pocket was closed, a breakout in that direction would still have been possible, but despite the personal intervention of the army group commander, Hitler did not change his mind. The pocket was to be held, and should only be relieved by a push from the west.

With no reinforcements in sight, the troops required for this relief thrust could only be taken from other sectors of Army Group Center, all of which had been severely drained in an attempt at strengthening Ninth Army at Rzhev. The direction for the attack was to be from southwest to northeast with the so-called citadel - a part of Velikiye Luki west of the Lovat River - designated as the primary objective. (Map 3)

It was obvious that LIX Corps, already responsible for an excessively wide sector of the front, could not be expected to take on the additional task of conducting this attack. The situation not only called for the use of fresh combat units but also for the establishment of a new tactical headquarters to direct the proposed relief operation. Unable to pull out a corps headquarters from any other sector, army group had to resort to an improvisation. A provisional corps headquarters, Corps Woehler, was formed under the command of the army group chief of staff assisted by the army group training officer, the chief artillery officer, and another young staff officer. Subordinate to LIX Corps which remained responsible for supply and administration, the newly formed command group was ready to take charge of the front sector opposite Velikiye Luki by mid-December. Its command post, established on 15 December at Lovno, was no less improvised than the staff by which it was occupied. A one-room peasant hut had to serve as living and working quarters for six officers, three clerks, three drivers, and two orderlies.

The terrain designated for the attack was desolate, rolling country, virtually without forests. Here Stalin's scorched earth policy had been fully effective in the Russian retreat of 1941.

Subsequent partisan operations completed the work of destruction. Most of the formerly inhabited places had vanished and even their last traces were now blanketed by heavy layers of snow. No roads or recognizable terrain features broke the monotony. Orientation was extremely difficult and at night a matter of pure chance. The entire area gave the impression of a landscape on the moon.

The German units initially available for the attack were a division from East Prussia, the 83d Division minus elements inside Velikiye Luki, the mountain regiment that had escaped encirclement south of the city, and two construction battalions. They had been weakened by considerable losses in men and materiel and were suffering from the effects of heavy frosts alternating with sudden thaws. Although their morale appeared unbroken, their combat value was definitely limited. Fortunately, their new commander, because of his experience as army group chief of staff, had no difficulty in finding out at what depots in the army group area ammunition and equipment could still be obtained. With railroads and transport planes doing their part, it took only a few days for the troops to be resupplied and re-equipped with new winter clothing. This brought about a rapid decline in the number of cold weather casualties.

Reinforced by a motorized division, a battalion of light infantry, two batteries of 105-mm. guns, and a rocket projector brigade, the improvised corps continued its preparations for the attack. They had to be cut short, however, since Hitler advanced the attack date by several days despite all objections by army group. The attack was launched shortly before Christmas but, after making good progress at first, bogged down at the half-way mark.

By now it had become clear that additional forces of considerable strength would have to be brought up in order to achieve success. The reinforcements finally made available consisted of two divisions and one tank battalion. At least one of these divisions, however, proved wholly inadequate for the type of operation in which it was to participate. Originally used as an occupation unit in western Europe, it had recently been transferred east and employed as a security force on a quiet sector of the Russian front. Two of its regimental commanders were considerably over-age and incapable of leading their units in combat. The third regimental commander, who was still in good physical condition, actually had to command each of the three regiments in turn as they were successively committed in the attack.

Army group had requested the approval of the Air Force for the employment of a parachute division which was then in a quiet position southeast of Velizh. *[Ed.: In the German system of organization, parachute units were part of the Luftwaffe.]* Goering refused, insisting that the division remain intact in its present position. Undoubtedly this refusal was one of the chief reasons why the liberation of Velikiye Luki failed.

The second German relief thrust was launched early in January 1943. Leading elements advanced to less than five miles from the northwestern outskirts of the beleaguered city. (Map 3) At that stage, however, enemy pressure against the long flanks of the penetration forced the Germans to assume the defensive.

Inside the pocket, the citadel on the left bank of the Lovat River had meanwhile become the refuge for some 500 wounded from all parts of the city. On 5 January the Russians attacked from the north and succeeded in cutting through the town and severing the citadel from the main part of Velikiye Luki. Thus two separate pockets came into existence, each one precariously defended after the loss of all positions beyond the edge of the town, and particularly threatened by enemy attempts at infiltrating from block to block.

Liberating the main German force encircled in the eastern part of Velikiye Luki had become even more difficult. In any event, the immediate objective was to cut through the ring of encirclement that surrounded the smaller pocket west of the river. A general advance of the corps front, however, as demanded by Hitler, was by now definitely out of the question.

After lengthy negotiations the Air Force finally released one battalion of its parachute division for commitment at Velikiye Luki. It was too little and too late, but a last attempt had to be made to open a rescue corridor to the citadel. In order to bolster the fighting strength of the encircled garrison, a reinforced company of light infantry riding on trucks and tank destroyers was to ram its way through the enemy into the surrounded citadel. On 10 January, in a daring daylight attack, this force took the Russians by surprise and succeeded in joining the German defenders inside the pocket.

During the night of 14-15 January, the parachute battalion was to advance in a surprise attack to the southwest side of the citadel. There, by 0100, the fresh troops recently arrived in the pocket were to attempt a breakout, taking with them all wounded who were still able to march. Although initially led by a regimental commander familiar with the area, the parachute battalion lost its way in the featureless terrain and failed to reach its objective. The citadel force broke out nevertheless, and in the early morning hours, reduced by casualties to about 150 men, appeared at the corps' advance command post on the Novosokolniki-Velikiye Luki railroad line.

By now, irreplaceable losses in the ranks of the German relief force made it impossible to repeat the rescue attempt. Also, no more radio signals were coming from the eastern part of Velikiye Luki - a clear indication that in six weeks of relentless fighting, despite the most determined resistance, the German force in the eastern pocket had been wiped out to the last man. The pocket commander's final radio message, received on 14 January, was, "With last strength and ammunition still holding two bunkers in center of city. Enemy outside my command post."

The struggle for Velikiye Luki was over. While it had the erect of tying down a greatly superior and constantly growing enemy force for six weeks, it also resulted in the annihilation of the German garrison, exorbitant casualties among the relief forces, and a loss of terrain along the entire corps sector. (Map 3) The important Nevel-Novosokolniki-Nasva railroad line still remained in German hands, free from enemy interference. However, the plan proposed by army group would have assured the same result without necessitating the futile struggle for Velikiye Luki. At the end of this ill-fated operation German casualties amounted to 17,000 officers and men, 5,000 of whom perished in the beleaguered city, while 12,000 were lost in rescue attempts from outside. Even if the relief thrust had eventually succeeded, the cost was far too high.

The experiences gained at Velikiye Luki might be summarized as follows:

1. Wherever a pocket comes into existence, it is usually the result of the attacker's numerical superiority over the encircled force. The deliberate adoption of a pocket-type defense can only be justified when early relief is assured; otherwise it will lead to the loss of the entire pocket force, and thus to a further decrease in the over-all fighting strength of the forces in the field.

2. The enemy's effective military strength, his combat troops, is his principle means of waging war. It must be destroyed. To fight constantly for terrain features, industrial installations, or simply for propagandistic purposes is to violate the basic principles of warfare.

3. It was Hitler who originally pronounced: "I must hold all pockets to the last in order to tie up superior enemy forces as long as possible." This may be correct in exceptional cases, but can never be elevated to the level of a general principle.

4. If an encircled force must be liberated by a relief thrust from the outside, only the best troops should be used in that operation. The more rapidly such a mission is completed, the fewer will be the casualties, and the greater the success. The

maintenance for any length of time of a long, narrow salient obviously pointing at the pocket will involve murderous casualties. In the end such tactics are almost certain to fail because of the pressure exerted by the enemy on both flanks of the salient.

5. Speed is an absolute requirement, but should not be gained at the cost of hasty and inadequate preparations. The selection and assembly of the relief forces involves careful deliberation and considerable effort. In the situation described, the supreme commander, on whose specific order the date for the attack had been moved up, was far away from the fighting front, and the effect of this intervention proved disastrous. There was nothing to justify such lack of confidence in the judgment of the local commander or in the recommendations of army group.

6. Constant communication with the encircled forces was maintained via radio which functioned smoothly and met all requirements. On several occasions the artillery fire of the relief force was actually directed by observers inside the pocket. Shuttle flights by liaison aircraft were possible only in the beginning, and then only at night.

7. Having the light infantry unit break out of the citadel at night proved to be a wise decision. Direction toward the forward elements of the rescue force was maintained with the aid of prismatic compasses. Advancing in several single files, the men succeeded in inching their way forward through the hollows and silently overpowering the Russian sentries.

8. Supply of the German pocket was at first effected from reserve stocks available at Velikiye Luki. Soon, however, airdrops became necessary, marking the first occurrence of a situation that was later so characteristic of all German pockets in Russia - the plight of encircled forces, inadequately supplied with ammunition, rations, and equipment, who were expected to do their utmost in a hopeless situation. If Hitler himself had ever been an eyewitness to such developments, Goering's

arrogant promises of adequate air supply for German pockets might have been discounted once and for all. The Luftwaffe units concerned were not in any way to blame. The missions assigned to them proved impossible of fulfillment, but they did their duty again and again in a superior manner, at Velikiye Luki, as well as at Stalingrad, and in all subsequent cases where German ground troops found themselves in hopeless encirclement.

THE POCKET WEST OF CHERKASSY - THE INSIDE VIEW

Section I.
EVENTS LEADING TO THE FORMATION OF THE POCKET

By the end of December 1943 - with Kiev (Reference Map) retaken by the enemy and a Russian bulge extending as far west as Zhitomir - the German forces in the Dnepr bend were ordered to hold their positions at all costs. XLII Corps (Map 4), on the right flank of First Panzer Army, had been under persistent enemy attack since 26 December when some of the Russian forces recently engaged in the battle for Kiev were shifted south and renewed their pressure against the corps sector. To the right, Eighth Army's XI Corps, the 5th SS Panzer Division Wiking as its left flank, was likewise engaged in heavy defensive fighting along its entire front. Both corps had the specific mission of continuing to hold their front lines against superior Russian forces in order to assure a favorable base for a projected German counteroffensive. To the left of XLII Corps, VII Corps had been operating against the flank of the Russian bulge. Since about 20 December the corps had been attacking in a westerly direction, but without achieving any significant results.

The situation of XLII and XI Corps, their most advanced elements fighting along the Dnepr and their long exterior flanks inadequately secured, was certain to invite attempts by the enemy to encircle and annihilate both corps. As early as mid-December the commander of XLII Corps had requested authority to fall back behind the Ross River. This would have

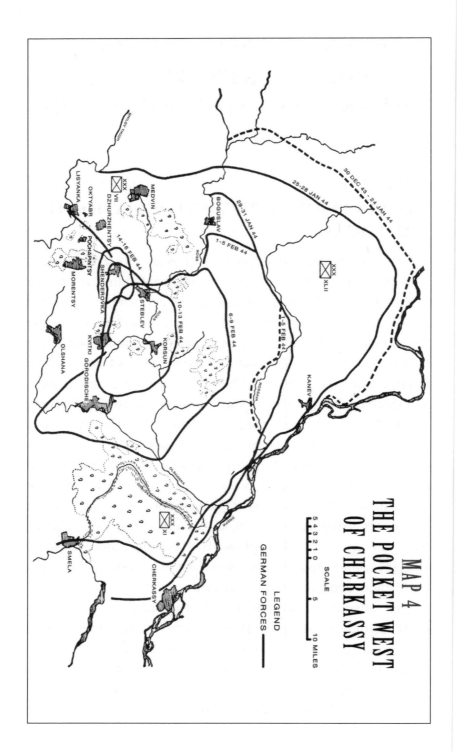

MAP 4
THE POCKET WEST
OF CHERKASSY

LEGEND

GERMAN FORCES ———

SCALE

5 4 3 2 1 0   5   10 MILES

30

meant that, instead of having to defend a frontage of seventy-five miles with two divisions, the corps would have been able to occupy a shortened defensive position behind a natural obstacle. However, that request was turned down.

Nevertheless, XLII Corps had taken a few precautionary measures during December. Two rear positions had been prepared north of the Ross River, east of Boguslav, which were to prove very useful later on in the withdrawal of the corps toward the south. Also, all food stocks of the former German civil administration in the corps area had been evacuated south of the Ross River, a move that turned out to be of decisive importance as these provisions soon became the sole source of supply for the German pocket forces.

Day after day, from the end of December 1943 until 24 January 1944, Russian infantry, often supported by tanks, attacked the positions of XLII Corps. From mid-January on the enemy's main effort was clearly directed against the left flank of the corps. On 25 January Soviet forces launched a large-scale attack against the adjacent VII Corps whose right flank division fell back toward the southeast and south, so that by the end of the same day the roads leading to the flank and rear of XLII Corps were open to the enemy. Over these roads the pursuing Russians pressed forward via Medvin toward Boguslav and Steblev.

Simultaneously, XI Corps had suffered enemy penetrations on the right boundary and at the center of its sector. To escape the danger of envelopment and keep its front intact, the corps withdrew its right wing and center toward the west and northwest where it was eventually to form the eastern front of the German pocket.

Before 24 January most enemy attacks against XLII Corps were blocked or repelled. These engagements, both in terms of battle casualties and lowered physical resistance of individuals, drained the fighting strength of the German forces. Their commanders were under constant pressure, trying to seal off the daily penetrations by virtually uncovering other sectors which were not under heavy attack and by using all available trucks, horses, and horse-drawn carts to shift their units to the threatened points. Initially, each of the two divisions on line with a troop strength of six battalions had to defend a frontage of 35 to 40 miles, with weak artillery support and without tanks. Except for the Ross River sector, the area in which they were committed was almost completely flat and offered few terrain features favoring the defense.

From mid-December 1943 until its breakout from the pocket on 16 February 1944, XLII Corps was actually never in a position to offer effective resistance to a far superior enemy who attacked with numerous tanks; if it could not dodge enemy attacks by timely withdrawal, it was constantly threatened by Russian penetrations of its lines. Authority for any withdrawal, however, could only be granted by Adolf Hitler in person, and no such decision could be obtained in less than twenty-four hours. One can easily visualize the difficulties, mounting from day to day, which the corps had to face under these circumstances.

The Russian attacks on 25 January and the following days had produced a deep penetration separating XLII and VII Corps. With its left flank and rear threatened by the enemy, XLII Corps was forced to establish a new front along the general line Boguslav-Steblev. For a short time it appeared that VII Corps would be able to close the gap and restore the situation, but after a few days, as the Russians succeeded in widening their penetration, it became evident that VII Corps was rapidly withdrawing toward the southwest. At this stage the German forces east of the Russian salient were ordered for the first time to make preparations for fighting their way out of the encirclement that was now taking shape. A breakout toward the west was clearly out of the question, thus southeast or due south were the only possible directions. During the first few days of February, however, another Russian penetration turned the right flank of XI Corps and made its position untenable. With its center withdrawing west and its right wing northwest the entire corps was rapidly moving away from its neighboring units adjacent to the southeast. In that area, too, a continuous German front had ceased to exist, and a breakout in that direction was no longer possible.

Moreover, since 28 January the sole supply roads leading to XLII; and XI Corps (via Shpola and Zvenigorodka) had been cut. Supply by air was requested and furnished. By 6 February, XLII and XI Corps were completely encircled.

In shifting its main effort toward the south, XLII Corps had been forced to weaken its northern and western fronts which were now slowly giving ground. This development, together with the withdrawal movements of XI Corps on the right, led to a gradual shrinking of the pocket, which in turn resulted in greater concentration - an important prerequisite for the eventual breakout from encirclement.

At the same time, it had become evident that the surrounded German units could escape annihilation only if they succeeded in breaking through the enemy lines on the southern front of the pocket. In weeks of defensive fighting, however, they had suffered excessive casualties, and the forces that would have to be used for such an operation were obviously incapable of getting through the Russian encirclement on their own; it was clear that the breakout attempt would have to be supported by a relief thrust from the outside. Accordingly, the encircled units were informed that III Panzer Corps, located about twenty-five miles southwest of the pocket, would launch an attack toward Morentsy in order to establish a forward rescue position. Simultaneously, another panzer corps at about the same distance due south of the pocket was to thrust north in the direction of Olshana.

On 6 February, in a radio message from Eighth Army, D Day for the breakout and rescue operation was set for 10 February. Because of the sudden start of the muddy season, however, the date had to be postponed for nearly a week. In order to establish unity of command inside the pocket, the two encircled corps were placed under the control of General Stemmermann, the commander of XI Corps, and designated Force Stemmermann.

Meanwhile, repeated Russian attacks - from the southeast against Korsun and Shenderovka, and from the west against Steblev - had threatened to split up the German pocket. Although all of these enemy thrusts were repelled, they further reduced the forces available for the breakout and had a detrimental effect on the morale of the encircled troops.

On 14 February elements of XLII Corps succeeded in taking Khilki and Komarovka (Map 5), two to three miles west of Shenderovka, and thus reached a favorable jump-off line for the final break-through. It was high time indeed: The gradual restricting of the pocket had resulted in a dangerous massing of troops. The entire German-held area was now within range of the Soviet artillery; volume and intensity of enemy fire seemed to be merely a question of how much ammunition the Russians were willing to expend. It was feared that at any moment German casualties might amount to an unbearable level. The Russians themselves, however, were hampered by snowstorms and poor road conditions and could not use their artillery to full advantage. Thus the German troops inside the pocket were able to rally for their last effort.

The breakout began, as ordered, on 16 February at 2300. Jumping off from the line Khilki-Komarovka, three divisional columns struck in a southwesterly direction; their mission was to reach the forward rescue position established by the leading elements of III Panzer Corps at Lisyanka and Oktyabr, and to join forces with First Panzer Army.

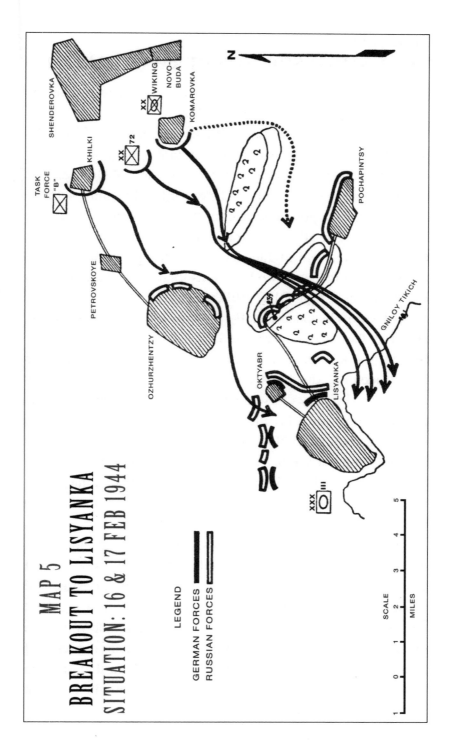

MAP 5
BREAKOUT TO LISYANKA
SITUATION: 16 & 17 FEB 1944

LEGEND

GERMAN FORCES

RUSSIAN FORCES

SCALE

MILES

SHENDEROVKA

WIKING

NOVO-
BUDA

KOMAROVKA

KHILKI

TASK
FORCE
"B"

72

PETROVSKOYE

OZHURZHENTZY

POCHAPINTSY

GNILOY TIKICH

OKTYABR

LISYANKA

239

Section II.
THE UNITS INSIDE THE GERMAN POCKET

The composition of the two German corps encircled in the pocket west of Cherkassy was as follows:

XI Corps consisted of three infantry divisions, the 57th, 72d, and 389th Divisions, each without tanks, assault guns, or adequate antitank weapons. Of these only the 72d Division was capable of aggressive combat. The two other divisions, with the exception of one good regiment of the 57th, were unfit for use in the attack. The 5th SS Panzer Division Wiking was part of XI Corps until the end of January. Corps troops comprised one assault gun brigade of two battalions totaling six batteries, and one battalion of light GHQ artillery.

XLII Corps included Task Force B, the 88th Infantry Division, and, from the end of January, the SS Panzer Division Wiking. Task Force B was a cover name given to the 112th Infantry Division to hide its identity. Although the unit carried a corps standard, it was an ordinary infantry division consisting of three regiments, the normal complement of artillery, a strong antitank battalion, but no tanks or assault guns. Now at about four-fifths of its authorized strength, Task Force B had the combat value of one good infantry division. The 88th Division had been badly mauled during the preceding engagements. It consisted of two regiments totaling five battalions and its artillery was seriously depleted.

In terms of personnel, weapons, and equipment the 5th SS Panzer Division Wiking was by far the strongest division of XLII Corps. It was fully equipped as an armored division and consisted of two armored infantry regiments, one tank regiment with a total of 90 tanks, the Belgian volunteer brigade Wallonien organized in three battalions, and one replacement regiment of about 2,000 men. Accurate strength reports from that division could not be obtained; its effective strength before the breakout was estimated at about 12,000 men.

Section III.
DIARY OF THE COMMANDER OF XLII CORPS

The tactical situation between 28 January and 16 February, as described above, was modified by a number of developments inside the pocket. A record of these events is found in excerpts from the diary kept by the commander of XLII Corps up to the time of the breakout:

28 January

Communications to the rear along the road Shpola-Zvenigorodka have been cut. We are encircled. First Panzer Army to restore communication routes. Our defensive mission remains unchanged. Telephone request to Eighth Army: "Mission requires maintaining northeast front against strong enemy pressure. Russian advance against Steblev necessitates main effort on southern sector. Request authority for immediate withdrawal of northern and eastern fronts. This will permit offensive action toward southwest and prevent further encirclement and separation from XI Corps."

29 January

Radio message from Eighth Army: "Prepare withdrawal in direction Rossava up to Mironovka-Boguslav. Be ready to move by 1200 on 29 January upon prearranged signal. Authority for further withdrawal likely within twenty-four hours. Report new situation."

Requested additional ammunition for artillery and small arms. Food supplies in the pocket are adequate. XI Corps under attack by strong Russian tank forces. Several of its regiments reduced to 100 men. Air supply beginning to arrive. Evacuation of casualties too slow. More than 2,000 wounded have to be removed.

31 January

Message from Eighth Army: XLVIII Panzer Corps will attack on 1 February toward Lozovatka [three miles northwest of

Shpola] to relieve enemy pressure against XI Corps.

1 February

Daily losses 300 men. Fighter protection inadequate. Ammunition and fuel running low.

2 February

Air supply improving. Radio message from Eighth Army: "Withdrawal of north front approved. Prepare for main effort on eastern flank of south front. Vormann [general commanding XLVIII Panzer Corps] is continuing the relief attack from the south. Breith [general commanding III Panzer Corps] will attack 3 February from southwest."

3 February

Air supply continues to improve. Unfortunately several transport aircraft with wounded aboard were shot down on the return flight. Have requested that air evacuations be made at night only unless adequate fighter protection can be provided. Message from Army: "To strengthen southern sector, occupy proposed line without further delaying action at intermediate positions."

4 February

Made a determined effort to take Boguslav. Commander of Task Force B seriously wounded. Now all the division commanders are artillerymen, including the present SS big shot. The north front is tottering. Russian tanks today captured a medium battery of Task Force B that was firing from every barrel without being able to score a single hit. Evidently we have too few experienced gunners. By nightfall our line is restored. Daily ammunition expenditure of the corps 200 tons. Casualties still 300 per day. This cannot go on much longer. Have requested 2,000 replacements, also 120 tons additional ammunition per day.

5 February

Radio message from Eighth Army: "Prepare breakout for 10 February. Further instructions follow."

7 February

Radio message to Eighth Army: "Roads deeply mired. Will require more time for breakout preparations." Message from Eighth Army: "At time of breakout the following units will attack from the outside: XLVIII Panzer Corps toward Olshana, III Panzer Corps toward Morentsy. Pocket force will effect initial break-through and, covering its flanks and rear, concentrate its entire strength in attack across the line Shenderovka-Kvitki toward Morentsy, to link up with armored wedge of relief forces. Regrouping must be completed in time to permit breakout on 10 February. Final decision will depend on progress of armored spearheads. Situation does not permit further delay."

Stemmermann *[general commanding XI Corps]* assumes command of both corps in the pocket. Report to Army that because of road conditions attack impossible before 12 February.

Had a look at the 110th Grenadier Regiment and Task Force B. Morale of troops very good. Rations plentiful. Enough sugar, sausage, cigarettes, and bread to last for another ten days. Army Group Commander radios that everything is being done to help us.

8 February

Radio message to Eighth Army: "Artillery, heavy weapons, and horse-drawn vehicles of 72d, 389th, and Wiking Divisions, as well as hundreds of motor vehicles of Wiking carrying many wounded, are stuck in the mud at Gorodishche. Withdrawal from line held today, to effect regrouping, would involve intolerable losses of men, weapons, and equipment. Line must be held at least twenty-four hours longer."

Today I saw many casualties, including four officers; ordered more careful evacuation of wounded, and destruction of all classified documents we can possibly get rid of.

9 February

Generals Zhukov, Konev, and Vatutin have sent an emissary, a Russian lieutenant colonel, who arrived with driver, interpreter, and bugler at the position of Task Force B to present surrender terms for Stemmermann and myself. He is treated to champagne and cigarettes, receives no reply. Ultimatum remains unanswered.

Forces for breakout dwindle from day to day. Inquiry from Army High Command about Leon Degrelle, commander of Brigade Wallonien. He is a young man, Belgian; I saw him a few days ago among his men. They are likeable fellows, but apparently too soft for this business.

Approach of relief forces delayed by necessary regrouping. Nevertheless Army now insists we break out on 12 February. Much as we would like to, we cannot do it by then. In this mud the infantry cannot possibly cover more than a thousand yards per hour.

10 February

My old division commander of 1940, General von Seydlitz [Ed.: Captured at Stalingrad by the Russians. Thereafter leader of the National Committee "Free Germany" composed of German officers in Russian hands.] today sent me a long letter delivered by aircraft: He thinks I should act like Yorck during the campaign of 1812 and go over to the Russians with my entire command. I did not answer.

Army inquires whether breakout in direction Morentsy still feasible, or whether the operation should rather be directed via Dzhurzhentsy-Pochapintsy toward Lisyanka. Reply to Army: "Lisyanka preferable if Breith [III Panzer Corps] can reach it. Situation on east front critical. Several enemy penetrations. For the past forty-eight hours XI Corps unable to establish new defense line. Troops badly depleted and battle-weary. XLII Corps front intact. We are attacking south of Steblev. Serious danger if east front cannot be brought to a halt. XLII Corps will break through in direction Lisyanka. The troops are well in hand. Early advance of Breith toward Lisyanka decisive."

Reply from Army: "Thanks for comprehensive information.

In full accord concerning new direction of breakout. Breith will attack 11 February in direction of Lisyanka. Will do all we can. Good luck."

Seydlitz today sent me fifty German prisoners with letters to their commanders; in addition they are supposed to persuade their comrades to go over to the enemy. I cannot understand Seydlitz. Although the events at Stalingrad must have changed him completely, I am unable to see how he can now work as a sort of G-2 for Zhukov.

12 February

Breith has reached Lisyanka. Vormann is advancing in direction of Zvenigorodka. Our infantry has taken the northern part of Khilki. [Map 5] The regimental commander leading the attack was killed in action. So goes one after another. XI Corps has taken Komarovka. The Russians, according to intercepted signals, are about to attack our left flank. Radio message to Army: "Absolutely necessary that Breith advance to Petrovskoye as quickly as possible, in order to effect link-up. Speed is essential. Forward elements of XLII Corps now at Khilki." Reply from Army: "Vormann southeast of Zvenigorodka. Breith will attack 13 February with strong armored wedge in direction Dzhurzhentsy."

Was at Khilki this afternoon. Things look bad. Our men are exhausted. Nothing gets done unless officers are constantly behind them. Am now keeping my horses inside the hut; they are in better shape than I. My orderly is burning my papers and giving away my extra uniforms.

13 February

Another message from General von Seydlitz, this time addressed to the commander of the 198th Division. Not bad: they think we are stronger than we really are. The letter was attached as usual to a black, red, and white pennant [German colors] and dropped from a plane. These people never fail to find my headquarters.

Breakout further delayed because of heavy enemy attacks against XI Corps' east front. Radio message to Army: "Concentration for breakout prevented by heavy Russian flank attacks and final mopping up at Shenderovka. Will shorten east front, involving evacuation of Korsun, during night of 13-14 February. Forces thereby released will not be available for breakout before 15 February. Intend to continue attack throughout 14 February. Breakthrough of Breith's armored force toward Petrovskoye indispensable to success."

Reply from Army: "Breith under orders to thrust toward Petrovskoye. His forward elements now on line Lisyanka-Khichintsy." Have requested strong fighter protection for 14 February. Russian strafing attacks are getting increasingly serious in view of the growing congestion in the pocket. I am most afraid that Army cannot comply with this oft-repeated request.

14 February

Breith will have to arrive soon. Last night the Luftwaffe dropped ammunition over the Russian lines instead of ours. Now they are trying to put the blame on us, claiming the drop point was inadequately lighted.

Stemmermann has just issued orders for the breakout. The date: 16 February. Radio message to Army: "North front will be withdrawn during the night of 14-15 February to the south bank of Ross River. Main attack ordered for 16 February. Further advance of tank force for direct support absolutely necessary."

We are destroying all excess motor vehicles and equipment. I have prohibited burning.

15 February

Our pocket is now so small that I can practically look over the entire front from my command post, when it is not snowing. Enemy aircraft are hard at work; lucky for us it is snowing most of the time. I was once more at Khilki to reconnoiter the terrain selected for the breakout. Then issued final order. Since this morning there is trouble at the SS Division. The Walloons and the Germania Regiment are getting fidgety. They must hold only until tomorrow night.

Final instructions from Stemmermann: We are to jump off on 16 February at 2300, with Task Force B. 72d Division, and SS Panzer Division Wiking from Khilki-Komarovka across the line Dzhurzhentsy-Hill 239 to Lisyanka; 57th and 88th Divisions will cover the flanks and the rear.

With me, at my command post, are the three division commanders with whom I am supposed to perform the miracle tomorrow. One of them is doing this for the first time, the two others are old hands.

I left no doubt in their minds that, in my opinion, this is going to be one giant snafu, and that they should not get rattled, no matter what happens. You need a guardian angel to bring you through this kind of thing.

Have given my second mount to my G-3. His Panje horse will be used by the G-2.

16 February

Ample supply of ammunition dropped in aerial delivery containers as late as last night. In this respect we are now well off - if we can take it along.

After consulting Stemmermann I decided to hand over to the Russians some 2,000 wounded together with medical personnel and one doctor from each division. This is a bitter decision, but to take them along would mean their certain death.

Saw Stemmermann once more to say good-bye. My orderly takes my diary; he is a crafty fellow and will get it through somehow.

Section IV.
BREAKOUT ORDER OF XLII CORPS

On the evening of 15 February, at his command post at Shenderovka, the commander of XLII Corps had issued verbal and written instructions to his division commanders. The breakout order for XLII Corps read, in part, as follows:

For days the enemy has been attacking continuously along our entire defense perimeter, with tanks and infantry, in an attempt to split up the pocket and destroy our forces.

At 2300, on 16 February, Task Force B. 72d Division, and 5th SS Panzer Division Wiking will attack in a southwesterly direction from the line Khilki-Komarovka, break the enemy's resistance by a bayonet assault, and throw him back in continuous attack toward the southwest, in order to reach Lisyanka and there to join forces with elements of III Panzer Corps. Compass number 22 [Ed.: The magnetic compass carried by the German soldier had 32 consecutively numbered gradations. Number 22 equals an azimuth of about 236°.] indicates the general direction of the attack. This direction is to be made known to each individual soldier. The password is: "Freedom" [Freiheit].

For the attack and breakout each division will be organized in five successive waves, as follows: First wave: one infantry regiment reinforced by one battery of light artillery (at least eight horses per gun, plus spare teams) and one engineer company. Second wave: antitank and assault gun units. Third wave: remainder of infantry (minus one battalion), engineers, and light artillery. Fourth wave: all our wounded that are fit to be transported, accompanied by one infantry battalion. Fifth wave: supply and service units.

The rear guard, under the direct command of General Stemmermann, will be formed by the 57th and 88th Divisions, which will protect the rear and the flanks of the forces launching the breakout attack. By 2300 on 16 February, the rear guard divisions will withdraw from their present locations to a previously determined defense line; further withdrawals will be ordered by General Stemmermann, depending on the progress of the breakout.

The entire medium artillery and certain specifically designated units of light artillery will support the attack. They will open fire at 2300 on 16 February, making effective use of their maximum range. Subsequently, all artillery pieces are to be destroyed in accordance with special instructions.

The radios of each division will be carried along on pack horses. To receive signal communications from corps, each division will, if possible, keep one set open at all times, but in any event every hour on the hour. The corps radio will be open for messages from the divisions at all times.

The corps command post will be, until 2000, 16 February, at Shenderovka; after 2000, at Khilki. From the start of the attack the corps commander will be with the leading regiment of the 72d Division.

The order was explained orally to the division commanders, and all details of the operation were carefully gone over, especially the difficult relief of the SS Division near Komarovka by the 57th Division, whose GO was present during the briefing conference.

Section V.
THE BREAKOUT

Despite persistent enemy attacks against the pocket perimeter, constant Russian shelling of Komarovka, Khilki, and Shenderovka, churned up roads, and numerous traffic bottlenecks, the German forces inside the pocket were able, by 2000 on 16 February, to report their readiness for the breakout. Determination was the prevailing mood. Apparently the large majority of the troops was not influenced by Russian propaganda, nor by the hundreds of leaflets dropped from Russian planes on behalf of the Free Germany Committee (General von Seydlitz) - they wanted to fight their way through.

Shortly after 2000, the commander of XLII Corps appeared

at the command post of the 105th Grenadier Regiment which was to spearhead the attack of 72d Division. He was on horseback, accompanied by members of his staff, several aides, and radio operators with their equipment. The events that followed are illustrated by a personal account of the corps commander, written from memory at a later date, and presented here in his own words:

By 2300 the regiment - two battalions abreast - started moving ahead, silently and with bayonets fixed. One-half hour later the force broke through the first and soon thereafter the second Russian defense line. The enemy was completely caught by surprise. Prisoners were taken along. Not until the following day did it become evident that the Russians, under the protection of heavy snowfall, had pulled out most of their troops from the south front of the pocket in order to use them in an attack, on 17 February, from the area west of Steblev.

The advance toward the southwest continued. No reports from either Task Force B on the right or the 5th SS Panzer Division on the left. That they were making some progress could only be inferred from the noise of vehicles due north and south of us, and from the sounds of firing that indicated the location of their leading elements. Over roadless, broken terrain traversed by numerous gullies, our march proceeded slowly. There were frequent halts. Here and there, men and horses suddenly disappeared, having stumbled into holes filled with deep snow. Vehicles had to be dug out laboriously. The slopes were steeper than could be presumed from looking at the map. Gradually the firing decreased until it broke off entirely by 0200. About two hours later the leading elements of 72d Division were approximately abreast of Dzhurzhentsy. Still no reports from Wiking and Task Force B. I could not give them my position by radio because by now my headquarters signal unit was missing and could not be located.

Shortly after 0400 enemy tanks ahead opened fire. They were

joined by Russian artillery and mortars operating from the direction of Dzhurzhentsy, at first without noticeable effect. The firing increased slowly but steadily, and was soon coming from the south as well. We began to suffer casualties. The advance, however, continued. By about 0600 the leading units reached a large hollow southeast of Dzhurzhentsy. Enemy fire, getting constantly heavier, was now coming from three directions. Elements of Wiking could be heard on the left, farther back. No message, and not a trace of Task Force B. Day was dawning. The difficult ascent out of the hollow began. The climb was steep and led up an icy slope. Tanks, guns, heavy horse-drawn vehicles, and trucks of all kinds slipped, turned over, and had to be blown up. Only a few tanks and artillery pieces were able to make the grade. The units lapsed rapidly into disorder. Parts of the Wiking Division appeared on the left.

Between 0700 and 1000 the 72d Division made several attempts to mount a co-ordinated attack toward southwest. It did not succeed. The few guns and most of the tanks that were still firing were soon destroyed by the enemy. Armored cars and motor vehicles suffered the same fate. Except for a few tanks that had managed to keep up, there were now only soldiers on foot and on horseback, and here and there a few horse-drawn vehicles, mostly carrying wounded.

In the protection of a ravine I was able to collect a small force of about battalion size, mainly stragglers from Task Force B and the Wiking Division. With them I moved on toward the line Hill 239-Pochapintsy, which was visible from time to time despite the heavy snowfall, and from where the enemy was firing with great intensity. Russian ground support planes appeared, opened fire, and disappeared again. They were ineffective, and did not repeat their attack, probably because of the difficult weather conditions.

There was no longer any effective control; there were no regiments, no battalions. Now and then small units appeared alongside us. I learned that the commanding general of the 72d Division was among the missing. My corps staff still kept up with me, but the aides who had been sent on various missions did not find their way back. On the steep slope northwest of Pochapintsy, defiladed from enemy fire, I found the G-3 of the 72d Division. He reported that infantry units of his division had penetrated the enemy line along the ridge south of Hill 239. Nevertheless, enemy fire was still coming from there, maintained principally by about ten Russian tanks.

Behind and alongside me thousands of men were struggling south-west. The entire area was littered with dead horses, and with vehicles and guns that had either been knocked out by the enemy or simply abandoned by their crews. I could not distinguish the wounded; their bandages did not show, as we were all wearing white camouflage clothing. Despite the general confusion and complete lack of control one could still recognize the determination in the minds of the troops to break through toward the southwest, in the direction of III Panzer Corps.

During a lull in the firing I readied my battalion for the attack across the line Hill 239 - Pochapintsy which unfortunately could not be bypassed. My staff and I were still on horseback. After leaving the draw that sheltered us against the enemy, we galloped ahead of the infantry and through the gaps between our few remaining tanks, The enemy tank commanders, observing from their turrets, quickly recognized our intention, turned their weapons in our direction, and opened fire. About one-half of our small mounted group was able to get through. The chief of staff and the G-3 were thrown, but later found their way back to us. The greater part of the infantry battalion was still following behind me. While riding through the enemy sector, I noticed a few German soldiers surrendering, but the main body was pushing southwest without letup. Soviet tanks were now firing at us from the rear and quite a few men were still being hit. From the eastern edge of the forest south of Hill 239 came intensive enemy fire. I led my battalion in an attack in that direction and threw the Russians back into the woods. Rather than pursue them into the depth of the forest, we continued advancing southwest, still harassed by fire from Russian tanks.

Gradually, between 1300 and 1500, large, disorganized masses of troops piled up along the Gniloy Tikich River, east of Lisyanka. Units from all three divisions participating in the breakout were hopelessly intermingled. A few medium tanks had been able to get through to the river bank, hut there were no heavy weapons and artillery pieces left. The river, below and above Lisyanka, was 30 to 50 feet wide, had a rapid current, and reached a depth of about 10 feet in most places. The banks were steep and rocky, with occasional shrubs and trees. Several tanks attempted to drive across, but the river was too deep and they failed to reach the opposite bank.

Heavy fire from Russian tanks located southeast of Oktyabr set the congested masses into forward motion. Many thousands flung themselves into the river, swam across, reached the opposite shore, and struggled on in the direction of Lisyanka. Hundreds of men and horses drowned in the icy torrent. An attempt by a small group of officers to create an emergency crossing for casualties succeeded only after several hours.

Toward 1600 the enemy fire ceased. I crossed the Gniloy Tikich swimming alongside my horse, traversed the snowy slope southeast of Lisyanka which was covered with moving men, and finally reached the town. There I found the commander of the 1st Panzer Division, the forward element of III Panzer Corps. I learned that no more than one company of armored infantry and three companies of tanks of 1st Panzer Division were now at Lisyanka, while one armored infantry battalion consisting of two weak companies was established at Oktyabr, the village immediately north of Lisyanka.

A reinforced regiment of Task Force B had made its way into Lisyanka, and I received the report that the commander of Task

Force B had been killed in action. Next, the chief of staff of XI Corps appeared; he had lost contact with General Stemmermann in the morning of 17 February, while marching on foot from Khilki to Dzhurzhentsy. He reported that the rear guard of the pocket force was in the process of withdrawal and that some of its units would soon appear.

I assumed command of what was left of Force Stemmermann. By now the situation was the following: The 72d and Wiking Divisions were completely intermingled. No longer did they have any tanks, artillery, vehicles, or rations. Many soldiers were entirely without weapons, quite a few even without footgear. Neither division could be considered in any way able to fight. One regiment of Task Force B was intact and still had some artillery support. However, this regiment also had no vehicles and no rations left. All wounded, estimated at about 2,000, were being gradually sheltered in the houses of Lisyanka, and later were evacuated by air.

For lack of vehicles and fuel, III Panzer Corps was unable to reinforce its units in the area of Lisyanka and Oktyabr. The corps commander, with whom I conferred by telephone, informed me that he had been forced to assume the defensive against heavy Russian attacks from the northwest in the area immediately west of Lisyanka. He had no extra supplies of any kind, and his forward elements were unable to provide rations for the troops emerging from the pocket. Thus I had to order the pocket force in its miserable condition to move on westward, while I requested supply, evacuation of casualties by air, and the bringing up of vehicles and weapons from the rear.

The march toward the main rescue area continued throughout the night, despite frequent bottlenecks, and was not completed until noon of 18 February. Renewed Russian flank attacks from the north endangered the roads to the rear and necessitated further withdrawal southwest and south during the following day. In the afternoon of 20 February, having clarified the question of food supply for the pocket force and dealt with a number of other problems, I was instructed to proceed to headquarters of Army High Command in East Prussia. From that moment on I had no further connection with XLII Corps or Force Stemmermann.

Of the 35,000 men launching the breakout from the pocket about 30,000 successfully fought their way out. 5,000 were killed or captured. The force lost all of its heavy weapons, artillery, tanks, vehicles, horses, equipment, and supplies.

THE POCKET WEST OF CHERKASSY - THE OUTSIDE VIEW*

Section I.
THE ENCIRCLEMENT

The second Russian winter offensive of 1943-44 was launched early in January 1944 against the German Eighth Army sector in the Dnepr bend. The First and Second Ukrainian Fronts - the latter consisting of four armies, including one tank army - attempted to cut off German forces deployed from a point southeast of Kiev to the Dnepr estuary. The Soviet offensive fell short of accomplishing its purpose, but in twelve days of fighting the Russians drove a deep wedge southwestward across the Dnepr and captured the town of Kirovograd. Two large German salients remained, one to the northwest, the other to the southeast of the Kirovograd area.

Despite heavy tank losses, the Russians could be expected to reorganize their armored forces in the shortest possible time and continue their heavy attacks designed to push Army Group South farther back in the direction of the Romanian border. It was evident that the enemy would bend every effort to destroy the German bulge northwest of Kirovograd, held by elements of Eighth Army and First Panzer Army.

The commander of Eighth Army sent urgent messages to army group; he expressed grave doubts about continuing to hold the

---

This description of the encirclement west of Cherkassy was prepared by a German staff officer at army group level on the basis of his personal recollections and is presented as a supplement to the preceding narrative.

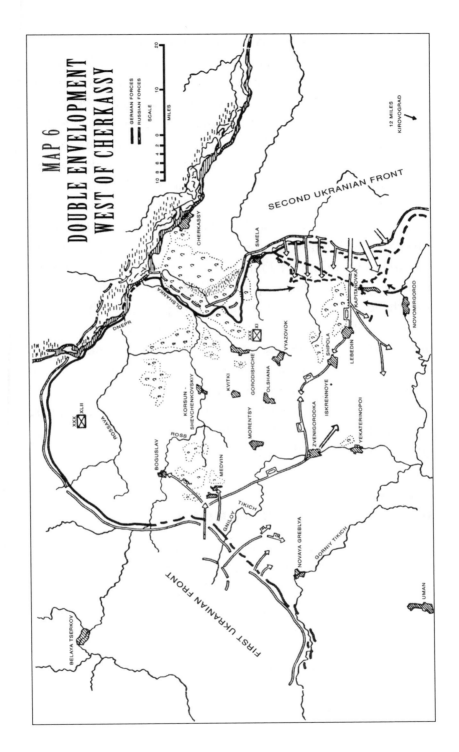

MAP 6

DOUBLE ENVELOPMENT
WEST OF CHERKASSY

curving line of positions northwest of Kirovograd which committed an excessive number of men. Pointing out the Russian superiority in strength, he recommended withdrawal of the interior flanks of Eighth Army and First Panzer Army by retirement to successive positions, first behind the Olshanka-Ross River line, and eventually to the line Shpola-Zvenigorodka-Gorniy Tikich River. Permission for such a withdrawal, however, was denied on the grounds that the salient had to be held as a base for future operations in the direction of Kiev.

The expected attack was launched by the Second Ukrainian Front, on 24 January, against the right flank, and by the First Ukrainian Front, on 24 January, against the left flank and the rear of the German salient. By 28 January the armored spearheads of both Russian army groups met in the area of Zvenigorodka and thereby accomplished the encirclement of XI and XLII Corps. Having erected the original link-up with elements of two tank armies, the Russians rapidly committed strong infantry units from four additional armies which attacked toward the west, southwest, and south in order to widen the ring of encirclement and provide effective cover against German counterattacks from the outside.

Section II.
PLANS FOR THE BREAKOUT

In this situation the German Army High Command directed Army Group South to assemble the strongest available armored units along the boundary between Eighth Army and First Panzer Army. These forces were to execute converging counterattacks, encircle and annihilate the enemy units that had broken through, re-establish contact with the pocket force, and regain a favorable jump-off base for the projected counteroffensive.

Actually, the assembly of the German attack force presented the greatest of difficulties. Two of the panzer divisions of Eighth

Army designated to take part in the operation were still in the midst of heavy fighting in the area of Kapitanovka. They had to be replaced by infantry units with frontages extended to the utmost. Two additional panzer divisions, recently engaged southeast of Kirovograd, were on the march toward the left flank of Eighth Army. Of these four armored units, only one was at full strength, while the others, after weeks of uninterrupted fighting, were actually no more than tank-supported combat teams.

The relief attack from the right flank of First Panzer Army was to be carried out by the four armored divisions of III Panzer Corps. They were still engaged in defensive operations on the left flank of the army sector, and could only be brought up after they had completed their previous missions.

The two corps inside the pocket were to attack at the appropriate time in the direction of the Eighth Army and First Panzer Army units approaching from the south and west. It was clear that any build-up on the southern front of the pocket could only be accomplished at the expense of other sectors. Still, Army High Command insisted on holding the entire pocket area, and not until the situation of the encircled forces became far more critical was permission obtained for successive withdrawals on the northern sector. Even then, the pocket had to be kept sufficiently large to afford a certain freedom of movement. Also, despite the effort on the southern sector, adequate forces had to remain available to seal off enemy penetrations elsewhere.

The plan for a two-pronged drive by III Panzer Corps of First Panzer Army from the southwest and XLVII Panzer Corps of Eighth Army from the south, to coincide with an attack launched by the pocket force, was adopted on 1 February. The units concerned were ordered to complete their assembly for the proposed operation during the following two days. Then XLVII Panzer Corps was to jump off from the area of Shpola, thrusting into the rear of the Russian forces that were threatening the

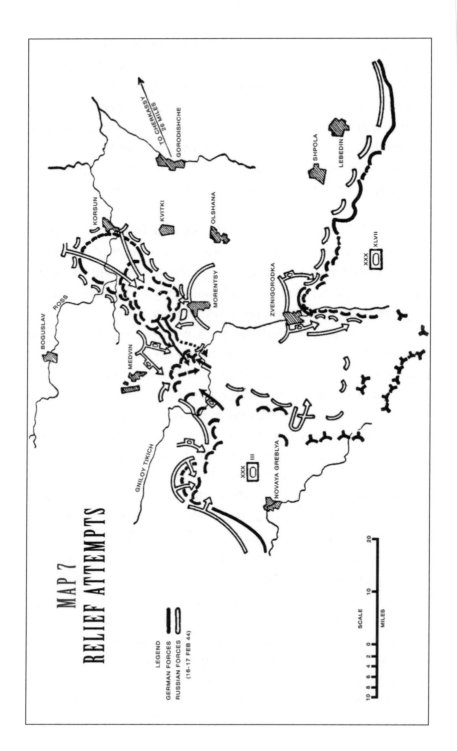

MAP 7
RELIEF ATTEMPTS

LEGEND
GERMAN FORCES
RUSSIAN FORCES
(16-17 FEB 44)

SCALE
10 8 6 4 2 0   10   20
MILES

TO CHERKASSY
26 MILES

GORODISHCHE

SHPOLA

LEBEDIN

KVITKI

OLSHANA

KORSUN

MORENTSY

ZVENIGORODKA

XXX
XLVII

BOGUSLAV

ROSS

MEDVIN

GNILOY TIKICH

NOVAYA GREBLYA

XXX
III

southern front of XI Corps. Simultaneously, III Panzer Corps was to launch a surprise attack in the general direction of Medvin, where enemy units were operating against the southwest front of the pocket defended by XLII Corps. After destroying these Russian units, III Panzer Corps was to pivot due east to effect close co-operation with the attacking elements of XLVII Corps coming from the south.

During a commanders' conference on 3 February, the Eighth Army commander voiced serious doubts whether, in view of the limited forces available and the muddy roads, this ambitious plan was practicable. He recommended instead that the attack by III Panzer Corps be led in a more easterly direction which would assure early co-operation with the advancing elements of XLVII Panzer Corps. This recommendation was turned down.

Meanwhile, the enemy had committed strong infantry and armored units in an attack toward Novomirgorod, temporarily tying down two of the panzer divisions that were to take part in the relief operation from the south. The muddy season was rapidly taking effect and as the roads deteriorated all movements became extremely difficult.

Similar conditions prevailed in the area of III Panzer Corps. Engaged in continuous fighting on its left flank, this corps also suffered considerable delay in the assembly of its units for the projected relief thrust and could not be expected to launch its attack until 4 February.

The forces inside the pocket, in an attempt to keep the enemy from separating XI and XLII Corps, had shifted their main effort to the south front of the perimeter. Despite heavy losses in defensive engagements they could not afford to give ground in that sector, as their only remaining airfield, at Korsun, had to be kept out of range of the Russian artillery. At the high rate of casualties, however, a continued stand along the entire perimeter of positions was obviously out of the question. To conserve its strength and reduce the threat of Russian penetrations, the pocket force eventually obtained permission to execute limited withdrawals on the northern and eastern sectors while bolstering its defenses to the south.

The full impact of the muddy season soon made itself felt on all fronts and, in addition to causing losses of motor vehicles and other equipment, began to endanger German air supply operations. The requirements of the encircled force called for supplies to be flown in at the rate of 150 tons daily. Despite the most determined efforts of the Luftwaffe units, this quota was never reached. Enemy antiaircraft fire from at least three flak divisions in the Russian-held strip of terrain and interception by enemy fighter planes had seriously reduced the number of available transport aircraft. To prevent further losses, strong German fighter forces had to be committed in protection of the vital air supply line instead of supporting preparations on other sectors for the impending relief operation.

With the start of the muddy season, the lack of paved runways further aggravated the situation. One airfield after another became unusable, and even the Korsun field, the only one inside the pocket, had to be partially closed. Airdropping supplies, because of a shortage of aerial delivery containers, met only a small part of the actual requirements. Eventually, because of the road conditions, the two corps approaching from the outside also became dependent in part upon airborne supply, which forced a wide scattering of the air effort.

Time was obviously working against the Germans. As their difficulties continued to increase, it became clear that each day of delay further reduced their chances for success.

Section III.
THE RELIEF OPERATION

The assembly of an attack force on the western flank of XLVII Panzer Corps (Eighth Army) bogged down in a series of heavy local counterattacks south of Lebedin and Shpola. A small German force gained a temporary bridgehead at Izkrennoye and inflicted serious losses on the enemy. In all these engagements, however, the strength of XLVII Panzer Corps was constantly being whittled down until, by 3 February, it had only 27 tanks and 34 assault guns left. At that point it became clear that Eighth Army could do no more than to tie down enemy forces by continued holding attacks. Thus the original plan which provided for two converging relief thrusts had to be abandoned.

Neverthless, on 4 February, First Panzer Army attacked toward the north in order to take advantage of favorable tank terrain, achieve surprise, and avoid any further loss of time. Successful during the first day, it was, however, unable to maintain this direction of attack, as terrain and road conditions grew worse by the hour.

Meanwhile, the situation inside the pocket had become more critical and made it imperative to establish contact with the encircled forces over the shortest possible route. Therefore, on 6 February, Army Group South issued new orders to First Panzer Army. After regrouping its units III Panzer Corps was to attack due east, its right flank advancing via Lisyanka toward Morentsy. At the same time the encircled corps were ordered to prepare for an attack in the direction of III Panzer Corps, the attack to be launched as soon as the armored spearhead of the relief force had approached to within the most favorable distance from the pocket.

Planned for 8 February, the attack of III Panzer Corps, because of unfavorable weather conditions, did not get underway until three days later. It was initially successful and, by the end of the first day, led to the establishment of three bridgeheads across the Gniloy Tikich River. Concentrated enemy attacks, however, prevented any further advance. In the difficult terrain east of the Gniloy Tikich, the German armored units were unable to make any progress, and this attack also came to a halt in the mud.

Army group now realized that it could no longer accomplish a reinforcement of the pocket. The encircling ring, therefore, had to be broken from the inside. The divisions of III Panzer Corps were ordered to engage and divert the Russian forces located in the area of Pochapintsy-Komarovka-Dzhurzhentsy, and to establish on the high ground northwest of Pochapintsy a forward rescue position that could be reached by the units breaking out of the pocket.

By 1105, on 15 February, the breakout order was transmitted by radio to General Stemmermann, the commander of the encircled German forces. It read, in part, "Capabilities of III Panzer Corps reduced by weather and supply difficulties. Task Force Stemmermann must accomplish break-through on its own to line Dzhurzhentsy-Hill 239 where it will link up with III Panzer Corps. The breakout force will be under the command of General Lieb [XLII Corps] and comprise all units still capable of attack."

Further instructions, radioed on 16 February, emphasized the importance of surprise and proper co-ordination: "During initial phase of operation tonight hold your fire so as to achieve complete surprise. Maintain centralized fire control over artillery and heavy weapons, so that in the event of stronger enemy resistance, especially at daybreak, they can be committed at point of main effort in short order. Air support will be available at dawn to protect your flanks."

Section IV.
THE BREAKOUT

During the operation that was to follow, two separate phases could be clearly distinguished. At first everything went according to plan. In the proper sequence and under perfect control, the troops moved into position at night, despite the most difficult road and weather conditions. As they were compressed into a narrow area, unit after unit had to be channeled across the only existing bridge at Shenderovka which was under heavy enemy fire.

The bayonet assault started on schedule. The complete surprise of the enemy demonstrated that the attack had been properly timed. Without much action, and suffering but few casualties, the German breakout force penetrated the enemy lines and in a relatively short time reached the vicinity of Lisyanka. On the opposite front of the pocket the rear guards held fast and thus assured the success of the initial breakout.

The second phase, the evacuation of the remaining pocket force, rapidly deteriorated into a wild surge toward the west. Following closely behind the successful spearhead, altogether about 30,000 men broke through the Russian lines in front of the pocket. At daybreak, however, they ran into an unsuspected enemy front of antitank guns, tanks, and artillery, located on the line Dzhurzhentsy-Pochapintsy. Under massed enemy fire, enemy tank attacks, and infantry counterthrusts, the German force was split into numerous small groups, each attempting on its own to get through to the west wherever there might be a possibility. Their guns, tank destroyers, and heavy weapons, which up to now had been dragged along laboriously through snowdrifts and over broken terrain, had to be left behind and were destroyed after the last round of ammunition had been fired. Here too, as the last vehicles were blown up, the wounded taken along at the insistence of their comrades had to be left to their fate.

Meanwhile a new complication arose that was to have disastrous consequences. Subjected to heavy enemy fire, counterthrusts, and armored attacks, the great mass of German troops breaking out of the pocket had deviated from their original direction of attack. No longer did they advance according to plan toward the area northwest of Pochapintsy.

Instead of approaching the forward rescue position established by III Panzer Corps, they passed by at a considerable distance farther south. Here, their advance to the west was blocked by the course of the Gniloy Tikich, the enemy holding the near bank of the river. There were no crossings, nor had III Panzer Corps established any bridgeheads, since a link-up in that area had not been foreseen.

Although greatly exhausted, the German troops were now forced to overcome the resistance of the Russian security detachments along the river and to swim across, leaving their last weapons behind. They suffered considerable losses as both banks of the river were under heavy enemy fire and not until they had placed this last obstacle behind them were they finally received by the forward elements of III Panzer Corps.

The German holding forces on the eastern sector of the pocket maintained contact with the enemy and successfully covered the breakout of the main body. This mission accomplished, they made their way westward according to plan and entered the lines of III Panzer Corps during the night of 17-18 February.

Contrary to expectations, the breakout had to be executed without air support. Unfavorable weather conditions during the entire operation made it impossible for the air force to play its part in the liberation of the encircled units.

Section V.
LESSONS

The developments mainly responsible for the encirclement near Cherkassy and its serious consequences might be summarized as follows:

1. Only the insistence of Army High Command to hold the Dnepr bend northwest of Kirovograd led to the isolation of two German corps in that area. Despite repeated requests, permission for a breakout was not obtained until too late. The enemy had

grown too strong along the entire ring of encirclement, while the German pocket forces had been weakened to such an extent, through losses of personnel and equipment and shortages of supply, that they were forced to surrender their freedom of action and maneuver to the enemy.

2. The two German corps encircled by the enemy were the flank corps of two adjacent armies. Immediately after their encirclement, XLII Corps, heretofore part of First Panzer Army, was placed under the command of Eighth Army. While this assured unity of command inside the pocket, the same was not true of the relief operation in which forces under the command of two different armies were involved. The absence of a unified command on the army level made itself felt particularly as the need arose to co-ordinate the actions of the pocket force (Eighth Army) with those of III Panzer Corps (First Panzer Army).

3. The mission of III Panzer Corps on the day of the breakout was to divert and tie down those Russian units that blocked the path of the German troops emerging from the pocket. Because of terrain difficulties and shortage of fuel, the corps' forward elements failed to reach and occupy the commanding ground originally designated as forward rescue area. Thus the enemy was able to throw considerable weight against the German units breaking out. Also - as the breakout continued in an unexpected direction - the exercise of command in the relief force was not flexible enough to adjust to the changed situation and improvise a new forward rescue position along the Gniloy Tikich River. As a result, the pocket force remained virtually unassisted in its efforts at breaching the Russian lines and fighting its way out.

4. The Luftwaffe, as mentioned above, was prevented from taking any part in the operation; an effective means of support that had been counted on was thereby eliminated.

The two German corps succeeded, to be sure, in cracking the enemy ring and breaking out of the pocket; but they were so seriously weakened that they required a long period of rest and rehabilitation before they could again be committed on the Russian front. Their absence had an immediate effect upon the defensive effort of Army Group South which was trying to counter heavy Russian attacks aimed at a break-through in the Uman area. Soon the entire southern sector was split wide open and the German Sixth and Eighth Armies were pushed across the Yuzhny Bug (Ukrainian Bug River) into Romania.

ENCIRCLEMENT OF A PANZER ARMY NEAR KAMENETS-PODOLSKIY

Section 1.
THE ENCIRCLEMENT

In mid-February 1944 the front of the First Panzer Army extended across the western Ukraine along a general line north of Vinnitsa and Shepetovka, northeast of Ternopol. To the right, north of Uman, was the Eighth Army; to the left, the Second Army. After the two corps encircled west of Cherkassy had made their way out of the pocket (Ch. 4), the front remained quiet until the beginning of March, while the Russians were reorganizing and regrouping their units. Then strong concentrations of Soviet tanks indicated that the enemy was getting ready to resume his attempts at forcing a decision.

The first large-scale Russian attacks, on 4 and 5 March, were directed primarily against the Shepetovka and Uman areas. Because of their great numerical superiority, the Russians succeeded in denting the overextended German lines in many places. While timely German counterattacks on the left flank eliminated the threat of a breakthrough aimed at Proskurov, the enemy was rapidly gaining ground in the Uman area and succeeded, by mid-March, in pushing across the Ukrainian Bug River. Having driven a deep wedge into the German front, the Russians were in a position to threaten the right flank of First Panzer Army. Since there were no German reserves available to close the gap, First Panzer Army was forced to withdraw its entire right wing and establish a new defense line facing east.

Under the pressure of continued Russian attacks, planned withdrawals were also carried out on the central sector until the right flank of First Panzer Army was finally anchored on the northern bank of the Dnestr River east of Mogilev-Podolskiy.

On the left boundary of First Panzer Army, west of Proskurov, strong Russian armored units soon accomplished another breakthrough. On 22 March five armored corps followed by infantry poured south between the Zbruch and Seret Rivers, and two days later crossed the Dnestr in the direction of Chernovtsy. Since the enemy had also pushed across the river farther east, in the area of Yampol and Mogilev-Podolskiy, First Panzer Army was now contained in a large semicircle north of the Dnestr. Hitler's explicit orders prohibited any further withdrawal and eliminated the possibility of a more flexible defense which might have established contact with other German forces to the east or the west. As could be expected, the two Russian forces, after crossing the Dnestr, linked up under the protection of the river line in the rear of First Panzer Army. By 25 March the encirclement was complete.

As in all similar situations, the first threat to make itself felt came when the last supply lines into the German salient were cut. Until 25 March First Panzer Army still had one supply route open, which led south across the Dnestr bridge at Knotin and was protected by a strong bridgehead on the southern bank of the river. Over this route all staffs and units that could be dispensed with were moved to the rear, and every nonessential user of supplies and equipment was taken out of the pocket before the ring was actually closed. As soon as it became evident that no more supplies could be brought up, stock was taken inside the pocket. While ammunition and rations were sufficient to last for about another two weeks, fuel reserves were found to be critically low. First Panzer Army therefore immediately requested supply by air and restricted the use of motor vehicles to a minimum.

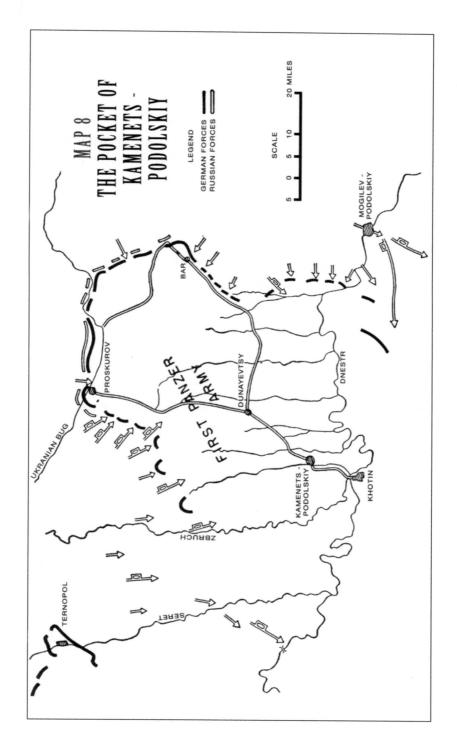

MAP 8
THE POCKET OF
KAMENETS -
PODOLSKIY

LEGEND

GERMAN FORCES
RUSSIAN FORCES

SCALE

5   0   5   10   20 MILES

TERNOPOL

SERET

ZBRUCH

UKRANIAN BUG

PROSKUROV

FIRST PANZER ARMY

DUNAYEVTSY

BAR

DNESTR

KAMENETS -
PODOLSKIY

KHOTIN

MOGILEV -
PODOLSKIY

All measures taken inside the pocket were made extremely difficult by unfavorable weather. At first snowstorms and snowdrifts hampered the air supply operation and obstructed movements on the ground. Then, practically over night, the snow began to melt, and the roads quickly turned into bottomless morasses. The supply of motor fuel, which was flown in over a distance of 125 miles from the nearest German airfield, fell far short of requirements. Time and again vehicles had to be destroyed when they blocked the roads in long, immobilized columns. Finally, only combat vehicles, prime movers, and a few messenger vehicles were left intact.

Having completed the encirclement the Russians, as expected, decreased the intensity of their attacks. Only on the eastern sector enemy pressure remained strong; there was no more than moderate activity in the north; and from the west no attacks were launched against the defense perimeter of First Panzer Army. Apparently the continuous movements of German service units southward across the Dnestr had led the enemy to believe that the First Panzer Army was in full retreat toward the south. The Russians, in an effort that turned out to be a serious mistake, moved more and more units in the same direction on both sides of the pocket. Their lines of communication grew longer and longer, and they began to face difficulties of supply similar to those of the encircled German force.

In response to enemy pressure from the east and north, First Panzer Army deliberately shortened its front until it ran along a much smaller perimeter north of Kamenets-Podolskiy, assuring a greater concentration of the defending forces and a more efficient use of the limited ammunition supply. Local enemy penetrations were sealed off more easily and break-throughs could be prevented altogether. At the same time First Panzer Army deceived the enemy into believing that by day and by night large-scale evacuations across the river were taking place.

Even before it was completely cut off, First Panzer Army had

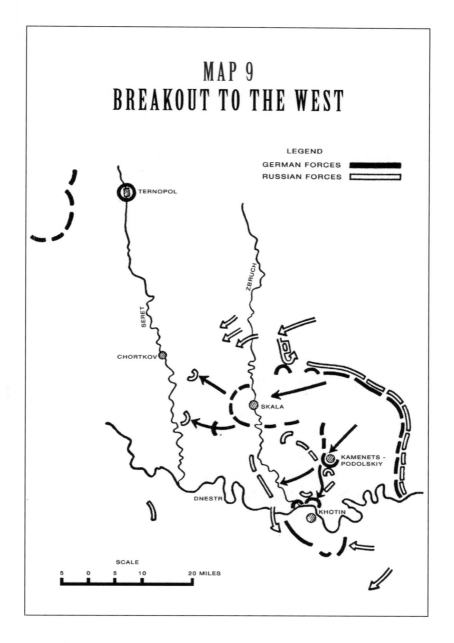

MAP 9
BREAKOUT TO THE WEST

LEGEND
GERMAN FORCES
RUSSIAN FORCES

TERNOPOL

ZBRUCH

SERET

CHORTKOV

SKALA

KAMENETS -
PODOLSKIY

DNESTR

KHOTIN

SCALE

5   0   5   10   20 MILES

requested authority to conduct a defense along mobile lines. When this request was turned down and the encirclement became a fact, a breakout remained the only possible course of action short of helplessly facing certain annihilation. Because of unfavorable weather conditions, the quantities of supplies that could be flown in were entirely insufficient to maintain the fighting power of the encircled troops. Relief of the pocket by fresh forces from the outside could not be expected. In this situation the enemy sent a terse demand for surrender, threatening that otherwise all soldiers of the encircled German army would be shot.

The reaction of First Panzer Army was to immediately make all necessary preparations to enable its total force of eight divisions to break out. Once more, in a systematic culling process, the divisions were relieved of all unfit personnel and superfluous equipment, while special arrangements were made with the Luftwaffe to assure that the transport planes bringing in supplies were used to evacuate casualties on their return flights.

Section II.
THE BREAKOUT PLAN

The question of the direction in which the breakout should be launched played an important part in all considerations. Was it more advisable to strike toward the west, along the Dnestr, or toward the south, across the Khotin bridgehead an attack in the latter direction would involve the least difficulties, be opposed by the weakest enemy forces, and perhaps permit the withdrawal of the entire German force into Romania. In this case, however, there would be one less panzer army fighting the Russians, at least for some time. West of the pocket several successive river lines constituted natural obstacles in the path of an advance. There, too, the Germans had to expect the strongest concentration of enemy forces along the ring of encirclement. Breaking out in several directions at once was another possibility under consideration; this would have forced the enemy to split his strength in numerous local countermeasures and might have enabled some small German groups to make their way back to the nearest friendly lines with the least fighting.

The final decision was to break out to the west, in the direction involving the greatest difficulties, yet assuring a maximum of surprise. Simultaneously, on the outside, another German force was to attack from an area southwest of Ternopol (over 125 miles from the scene) in the direction of First Panzer Army.

Another highly important question was the formation to be adopted for the breakout. Desirable as it might have been to lead off with a strong concentration of armor, it was to be feared that these armored units, intent on making rapid progress, might outrun the infantry and thus break up the unity of the command. The plan of attack, therefore, provided for a northern and a southern force, each consisting of two corps and specifically ordered to form an advance guard of tank-supported infantry and combat engineers, while the main body and the rear guard were to be composed of mobile units. This meant that the entire panzer army would be committed in two parallel formations attacking abreast, with units in column. Control over the operation, of course, could only be exercised from inside the pocket; evacuation of an operations staff via Khotin to the south, in order to direct the breakout from the outside, was out of the question.

Section III.
THE POCKET MOVES WEST

On 27 March, having regrouped its forces according to plan and completed all preparations for the thrust across the Zbruch River, First Panzer Army launched its breakout toward the west. Simultaneously, the rear guards on the eastern and northern sectors of the pocket switched to delaying tactics.

In the zone of the northern attack force, the enemy along the Zbruch River was overrun with surprising speed, and three

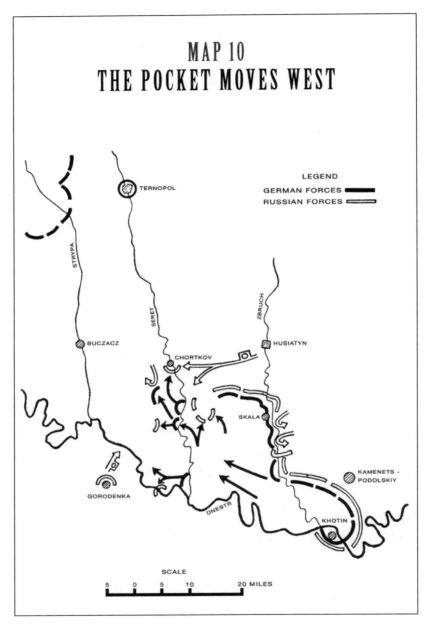

MAP 10
THE POCKET MOVES WEST

LEGEND
GERMAN FORCES ▰▰▰
RUSSIAN FORCES ▱▱▱

TERNOPOL

STRYPA

SERET

ZBRUCH

BUCZACZ

CHORTKOV

HUSIATYN

SKALA

KAMENETS - PODOLSKIY

GORODENKA

DNESTR

KHOTIN

SCALE

5 0 5 10   20 MILES

undamaged bridges fell into German hands. The advance of the southern attack force met greater resistance, and considerable difficulties arose as the enemy launched a counterthrust from the west across the Zbruch and was able to force his way into

Kamenets-Podolskiy. The loss of this important road hub made it necessary to reroute all German movements in a wide detour around the city, an effort that required painstaking reconnaissance and careful traffic regulation. It was not long, however, until the enemy penetration was sealed on, and in this instance the Germans, themselves surrounded, were able in turn to encircle a smaller Russian force which was not dependent upon air supply and could no longer interfere with subsequent operations. As soon as several strong bridgeheads had been established across the Zbruch River, new spearheads were formed which attacked the Seret River line. Thus the panzer army maintained the initiative and kept moving by day and night.

Apparently the enemy was still uncertain about German intentions. Instead of combining all his forces from the eastern and northern sectors in an attempt to pursue and overtake the Germans pushing west, he persisted in attacking the pocket from the east and north, in some instances striking at positions already vacated by the German rear guards. His units southwest of the pocket actually continued to move farther south. Meanwhile, First Panzer Army kept up its westward advance; on 28 March the southern force was able to cut the road leading to Chortkov, severing enemy communication lines in that area; one day later German spearheads reached the Seret River, which they crossed during the following night.

The Russians then began to react. They recalled elements of their Fourth Tank Army from south of the Dnestr and, by 31 March, launched a strong armored thrust toward the north from the area of Gorodenka. As a countermeasure, the southern attack force of First Panzer Army, deployed mainly between the Zbruch and Seret Rivers, assumed the defensive and was able to break up the Russian armored attack. Thereafter, since their supply lines had meanwhile been cut, these Russian units no longer constituted a menace to the German left flank.

A more serious threat existed in the north where Russian forces moving west could have overtaken and blocked the entire right wing of First Panzer Army. However, the enemy did not choose to do so, and the northern attack force continued to advance and was able to cross the Seret without major difficulty.

Section IV.
THE ESCAPE

The last week in March was marked by heavy snowstorms. A rapid thaw followed early in April, with the effect of seriously hampering all movements. Supply during this period continued to be the greatest problem. As the German force kept moving, the planes bringing in supplies had to use different airstrips every night. In the final phase of the operation supplies could only be dropped by air, a procedure that proved wholly inadequate to satisfy the requirements of an entire army. Despite the daily moves of the pocket force, the maintenance of adequate signal communications was assured at all times, primarily by the use of conventional and microwave radio sets.

Since the troops were constantly on the move, launching successive attacks toward the west, they never developed the feeling of being trapped in the slowly tightening grip of an encircling enemy force. Consequently, there were no signs of disintegration or panic, and the number of missing during the entire operation remained unusually low. By 5 April the leading elements of both the northern and the southern attack forces reached the Strypa River. On the following day, near Buczacz, they were able to link up with other German units coming from the west.

In two weeks of heavy fighting, but without suffering severe casualties, First Panzer Army had freed itself from enemy encirclement. Rear guard actions continued for a few days and then the Germans succeeded in establishing a new, continuous defense line running from the Dnestr to the town of Brody, which prevented any further advance of the enemy. Moreover, despite their considerable losses in materiel, elements of First Panzer Army were still able to launch an attack southeast across the Dnestr to break up an enemy force which had appeared in the Stanislav area. Enemy equipment captured and destroyed during the entire breakout operation amounted to 357 tanks, 42 assault guns, and 280 artillery pieces.

Section V.
EVALUATION

In its encirclement and breakout, First Panzer Army gained a number of experiences that may be applicable to many similar situations. Whereas in previous wars the double envelopment and encirclement of a unit was tantamount to its annihilation, this is no longer true today. The progressive motorization of ground forces, combined with the possibility of supply by air, tends to do away with this hitherto characteristic aspect of a pocket.

While it is true that the decision to break out from encirclement should not be needlessly delayed, it is equally important to realize that definite plans for the breakout should not be made too early, at a stage when the enemy is still moving and therefore capable of making rapid changes in his dispositions. Once the encirclement is completed, the enemy, since he is now operating along exterior lines, encounters difficulties of supply and communication and has lost much of his initial flexibility.

In an operation of this type surprise is the most important factor, particularly the surprise achieved by choosing an unexpected direction for the breakout. In the example described all movement prior to the encirclement of First Panzer Army had been from north to south. A breakout in the same direction was definitely expected by the enemy, and therefore this would have been the least favorable choice. The direction selected for the German thrust - practically perpendicular to the enemy's lines of advance - offered the best chance of success; the element of surprise actually proved of greater importance than considerations of enemy strength, terrain conditions, and the distance to the nearest German lines.

CONCLUSIONS

Section I.
THE SIGNIFICANCE OF A POCKET

In modern warfare with its blitzkrieg tactics executed by motorized and mechanized forces, the encirclement by the enemy of large bodies of troops has become a frequent occurrence. It is, therefore, all the more important to be adequately prepared for this kind of fighting.

Combat in pockets, whether it be of long or short duration, has its own fundamental rules. Whatever circumstances may determine the length of the battle, it will always be advisable to seek an early decision. To make this possible, the commander of an encircled force must, on principle, be granted full freedom of action. He should be permitted, specifically, to use his own judgment regarding all measures and decisions incident to a breakout from the pocket. On many occasions in German experience, the futile attempt was made to evaluate a local situation and to conduct the operations of encircled troops by remote control from a far distant higher echelon, if not directly from Hitler's headquarters. Indecisiveness on the part of the pocket commander and measures which invariably came too late were the consequences of such limitations imposed by higher headquarters. Whenever a commander receives rigid instructions from a distance at which the capabilities of his encircled forces cannot be properly judged - and are usually overestimated - his willingness to accept responsibility will rapidly decline.

The notion that pockets must be held at all costs should never be applied as a general principle. Hitler's adherence to this

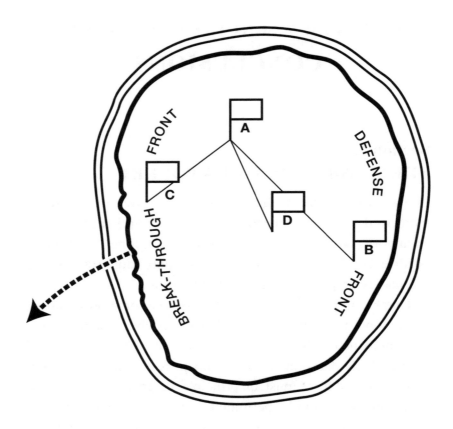

mistaken concept during World War II resulted in the loss of so many German soldiers that the lesson learned from their sacrifice ought to be remembered for all time.

Section II.
SPECIAL OPERATING PROCEDURES

Experience has shown that only seasoned troops, in the best fighting condition and under the firm control of their commanders, are able to withstand the mental strain of combat in encirclement and are likely to retain the high degree of physical fitness needed under such circumstances. But even with troops that satisfy these requirements it is necessary to apply stern measures in order to prevent any slackening of control, which would inevitably result in lowering their morale. It is surprising how fast the bonds of discipline will disintegrate in an encirclement. Mobs of unarmed soldiers trying to proceed on their own, captured horses loaded down with superfluous equipment, and other similarly depressing sights were not uncommon in some of the larger German pockets in Russia. They had a contaminating effect and called for swift and drastic countermeasures.

The highest standards of discipline, more important in this than in any other situation, must be upheld by the officers and noncommissioned officers of an encircled force; it is their personal conduct that sets the example. Force of character, as in all critical situations, acquires the greatest significance; it sustains the will to fight and may, indeed, determine the outcome of the battle. More than ever the place of the commander, under such circumstances, is in the midst of his troops; their minds will register his every action with the sensitivity of a seismograph.

Particular attention in all matters of discipline must be paid to rear echelon units and the personnel of rear area installations that may be present in the pocket. Since these troops are usually the first to become unnerved, they must be held under strict control.

Another principle that has proved itself in the German experience is the delegation of authority (see diagram) by the pocket commander (A) to three subordinate command elements within the pocket; one (B) to maintain the defensive effort; another (C) to prepare and conduct the breakout; and a third (D) to be responsible for organization, traffic control, and the maintenance of discipline inside the pocket.

Communication and co-ordination with other friendly forces, particularly in the case of a relief thrust from the outside, will have to remain among the exclusive functions of the pocket commander. Presumably, he alone will have the necessary radio facilities at his disposal. It is, of course, an absolute requirement, for the delegation of authority described above, that all the forces inside the pocket be under one command. Since envelopment attacks are usually directed against tactical weak spots, such as army or corps boundaries, uniform command over the forces encircled by the enemy is not always assured at first. It must be established as soon as possible; otherwise, as demonstrated in Chapter 4, considerable difficulties will be encountered in the defense of the pocket, as well as in the conduct of relief operations from the outside.

The tactical principles which, in an encirclement, apply to the various combat arms, may be summarized as follows:

1. Infantry

In the initial phase, during which the entire perimeter is to be held, everything up front! An encircled force can ill afford loss of terrain. Therefore, strong reserves must be held close by; the battle position must be a closely knit system of strong points with a well-co-ordinated fire plan for all infantry heavy weapons; and the outpost area must be kept under constant surveillance by reconnaissance and combat patrols, particularly during the night. If this cannot be accomplished because of inadequate forces, the perimeter should be shortened deliberately to the point where the defenses can be organized in accordance with the principles outlined above.

2. Artillery

In small- and medium-sized pockets the ordinarily undesirable bunching up of artillery units cannot be avoided. Here, however, it is of advantage in that it permits a rapid shift of fire, thus assuring direct support for large parts of the front without displacement to new positions. Also, centralized fire direction can be more easily established. A practice that proved particularly effective was the firing of a few batteries at a time, while the bulk of the artillery remained silent to avoid counterbattery fire. Massed artillery went into action only against large-scale enemy attacks.

3. Armor and Antitank Weapons

In the defense of pockets, tanks and assault guns have a dual mission. Contrary to the rules of armored combat under ordinary circumstances, they are scattered among the infantry and take part in the small-scale fighting along the perimeter. At the same time, they must be able to revert quickly to their original formation whenever they have to be used as mobile reserve against major enemy attacks. Similarly, the proper place for antitank weapons is with the front-line infantry. An antitank defense echeloned in depth, as is preferable in most other situations, must be ruled out for the same reasons that apply to the employment of the infantry.

The necessity for tight organization inside the pocket has already been emphasized. This applies particularly to traffic control which must be so enforced as to assure order and discipline, and to prevent panic. It may be necessary, for this purpose, to employ not only all available military police but also seasoned combat troops under the command of forceful and experienced officers.

All measures that must be taken inside a pocket will vary depending upon local circumstances; no two situations are alike. Therefore, set rules cannot be prescribed for fighting in pockets any more than for other types of military operations. Nevertheless, the fundamental principles outlined above seem to apply whenever troops are encircled by the enemy.

So long as the encirclement has not been completed - or before the enemy ring has been reinforced - an immediate break-through offers the best chance of success. Few tactical preparations will be necessary, if a command faced with encirclement can exploit the opportune moment by breaking out as soon as the enemy's intentions have been recognized. In most instances, however, all elements of the surrounded force will be locked in battle for several days, and the opportunity for such immediate action will pass before the situation in the pocket has become sufficiently clear. Then, especially in the case of larger pockets, a breakout can be launched only after the most careful preparations which must include some or all of the following considerations and measures.

Section III.
THE BREAKOUT DECISION

Unless the encircled forces have explicit orders to remain in place, or are so weak that they must rely on relief from the outside, the decision to break out must be made before the enemy has been able to forge a firm ring around the pocket. Only if this is done, and only if preparations are begun without delay, will all measures become part of one coherent plan, directed toward a single objective.

Such situations bring out the innate aggressiveness, flexibility; and initiative of a born leader. The need for quick decisions, however, must not be permitted to cause action without plan. The proper time and direction for the breakout, for instance, can only be determined after the following questions have been answered:

a. When - according to the tactical situation - is the earliest suitable moment for launching the attack?

b. Where is the enemy the weakest?

c. Which is the shortest way back to friendly lines?

d. What direction of attack would involve the least terrain difficulties ?

e. What time of day and what weather conditions are most favorable for the attack?

f. Should one or several directions be selected for the breakout?

The answers to these questions will vary according to the situation, as can be seen from the preceding chapters. Actually, there may be situations in which - contrary to the principles advanced above - the direction for the breakout should not be fixed too early, at least not until the enemy's intentions can be clearly recognized. (Chapter 5)

As a rule, unless the breakout is to be co-ordinated with the approach of a relief force from the outside, the units fighting their way out should follow the shortest route back to their own lines. In many instances the direction most favorable in terms of terrain and enemy resistance cannot be used if it does not permit a link-up with friendly forces in the shortest possible time. With troops in good fighting condition, the attack can be launched at night; if they are battle weary, the breakout must be made in the daytime, so as to obtain better control and co-ordination.

A breakout in several directions offers the least chance of success. It is attempted as a last resort, in order to obtain a greater dispersal of one's own forces, which might enable some small units to fight their way back to their own lines. Such an attempt is more or less an act of desperation - when relief from the outside cannot be expected, and the distance to the nearest friendly lines has become so great that it can no longer be bridged by the exhausted pocket force.

Section IV.
SPECIAL LOGISTICAL PREPARATIONS

A successful breakout is the result of sound planning and systematic preparation. It is also one of the most difficult combat maneuvers that a military force can be called upon to attempt. This fact must be taken into account in all preparatory measures. Prior to the breakout, for instance, the troops should be stripped of all unnecessary equipment, that is, of all equipment they might not need during the fighting of the next few days. This must be done without hesitation and without regard to their possible future requirements, should they have to be committed again after the breakout. The easier the lost equipment can be replaced afterwards, the less weight will be given to such considerations. German commanders in World War II were never allowed to forget that every weapon and vehicle was virtually irreplaceable - a typical sign of a "poor man's war." To some other nations, however, these limitations do not necessarily apply.

Until the pocket force is entirely surrounded by the enemy - but as soon as encirclement appears inevitable - the last open road must be utilized for the evacuation of casualties and of all nonessential staff sections, detachments, and service troops. If there is still time, excess weapons and equipment may be moved out over the same road. The commander should not fail, however, to make full use of this last opportunity to get rid of rear echelon troops; in an encirclement they are a greater burden than superfluous equipment, which can be destroyed if necessary.

Technical preparations in the pocket begin with what might be called the "big clean-up." All weapons that cannot be fully manned or adequately supplied with ammunition must be destroyed. The same is true of all heavy guns that might be a hindrance in view of expected terrain difficulties, as for instance all artillery pieces of more than 150-mm. caliber. As a rule, it is better to destroy one gun too many, than to drag along a single weapon that cannot be employed.

Similar principles apply to the destruction of motor vehicles. Exactly how many are to be destroyed will depend upon the availability of fuel and the requirements for the transportation of casualties and indispensable equipment; in any event, the majority of vehicles will have to be destroyed. Hardest hit by these radical measures are usually the supply services. Here, only a forceful officer in charge of destruction will be able to carry out his mission successfully.

Official papers are another victim of the general clean-up. Their destruction is a task that every soldier will undertake with fiendish pleasure. Files, administrative forms, voluminous war diaries, orders, regulations, and directives are consigned to the flames - the higher the classification, the greater must be the care taken to assure that they are completely destroyed. Only the most important papers, radio codes, and in some cases personnel files, may be left intact, so long as there is hope that they might be saved.

Effective traffic regulation is a prerequisite for all tactical moves inside the pocket. If an adequate road net exists, separate routes must be designated for the movement of supply units and combat troops, and even for armor and infantry. The Germans found it expedient to co-ordinate all traffic in a pocket by preparing a regular timetable that had to be strictly observed.

However, the problem of traffic regulation inside a pocket is not confined to troop movements. The most carefully devised system of traffic control can be upset by streams of fleeing civilians who are likely to be stricken with panic when caught in a pocket. As a rule, therefore, it is imperative for the security of the encircled force to prohibit and prevent any movement of local inhabitants. Only in rare cases will it be possible to take along part of the civilian population during a breakout. Then, while the roads are kept clear, special paths must be assigned for the treks of civilians. Particularly in large pockets, the question whether able-bodied male inhabitants should be taken along or left behind deserves careful consideration; it can only be decided on the basis of local circumstances.

Extensive preparations will also be necessary if an encircled force is to be supplied by air; these preparations are described in detail in the Appendix to this study.

Section V.
TACTICAL PREPARATIONS

In an encirclement a deliberate effort must be made to increase the effective strength of the combat element at the expense of the service units. Selecting the proper personnel to be transferred from rear echelon to combat duty may be a slow process, but it is of the greatest importance at a time when active fighters are needed more than anything else. In such situations, the service units - having grown out of proportion to the combat element - are largely superfluous and actually impose a heavy burden on the command. At best, they constitute a manpower reserve which, after a thorough process of selection, will yield additional personnel for combat duty. One should not expect too much of this reserve - while it is composed of military personnel, it will include few combat soldiers. Assigning an excessive number of rear echelon troops to front-line duty will only swell the numerical strength of the combat element without, however, increasing its fighting power to the same degree. The procedure completely loses its usefulness when the men transferred from service units are no longer a reinforcement of, but a burden to, the combat element. Rear echelon troops whose services have become superfluous and who can no longer be evacuated, should be placed in a single unit and held under firm control.

Demolitions, which are to prevent rapid pursuit by the enemy or to slow his exploitation of recently abandoned terrain, are to be ordered and executed in time; condemned artillery ammunition makes a good explosive for this purpose. It is advisable, however, to confine such demolitions to a few important objects. Experience has shown that as a rule the troops have neither the time nor the inclination to carry out extensive and time-consuming missions of destruction. On the other hand, the commander must take care to prevent senseless mass demolitions born of a spirit of destructiveness that is characteristic of encircled troops.

The success of a breakout will depend primarily upon the use of deception and the maintenance of secrecy. The fewer subordinate commanders informed about the actual breakout plan, the greater the chances that secrecy can be maintained.

Especially telephone and radio communications must be carefully guarded. At the same time, radio offers the best means for deceiving the enemy. This may be done by transmitting dummy messages about one's own intentions, calls to imaginary relief units, reports that will confuse the enemy about the actual strength of the pocket force, misleading requisitions for supplies, and false information about drop zones and landing areas. All these ruses are certain to reduce the number of casualties during the breakout.

Tactical feints and deceptive maneuvers must go hand in hand with the measures suggested above. By moving into different positions every night, launching attacks with limited objective from various points of the perimeter, and stubbornly holding on to unimportant terrain features, the encircled force must deliberately convey to the enemy a false picture of its situation and of its intentions. This purpose can also be served by having a sizeable column composed of all available supply units move laterally across the sector from which the breakout will eventually be launched.

Effective deception can always be achieved by concentrating armor at a point other than that of the intended breakout. If these tanks proceed to execute a feint attack, the enemy, believing that he has located the main effort of the breakout force, will almost certainly divert the bulk of his forces to the threatened point. The attacking tanks are then shifted rapidly into the direction of the main break-through, and success will usually follow. (Ch. 2) Such deceptive measures by tanks, depending of course upon the fuel situation, should be used both in the defense of the pocket perimeter and - as an ace in the hole - immediately before the breakout is launched. The desired result can often be achieved by having a single tank drive in circles at night to feign the assembly of a large armored unit. No matter what measures of deception are used, they will only serve their purpose if they enable the breakout force to take the enemy by surprise. In this respect the preparations for a breakout do not differ from preparations for any other type of attack. Here, as in any offensive action, secrecy, deception, and surprise are the basic elements of success.

The most important tactical preparations for the breakout - apart from diversionary attacks - are concerned with the gradual change of emphasis from the defense of the perimeter to the formation of a strong breakout force. As the situation permits, every soldier who can be spared from the purely defensive sectors must be transferred - possibly after a rest period - to the area selected for the breakout.

This will weaken the defense and, in some places, necessitate a shortening of the line which may involve considerable risks. Enemy penetrations are likely to occur, and such local crises, although they may have little or no effect upon the over-all situation, are usually overestimated by the commanders on the spot. These difficulties, of course, are greatly reduced if the entire pocket keeps moving in the general direction of the breakout. The necessary shifting of forces is then more easily accomplished, and minor losses of terrain on the defensive front are no longer regarded as serious setbacks. The advantage of a moving pocket in terms of morale is obvious. No claustrophobia will develop because the troops are spared the feeling that they are making a last stand in a pocket from which there is no escape.

During the defense of a pocket, local crises are a daily occurrence. The pocket commander and his staff must be ready at any moment to take the necessary countermeasures against serious emergencies. Actually, each passing hour may bring new surprises and call for new decisions, and it is not always easy to distinguish between important and unimportant developments. The commander must keep in mind that his reserves are limited and should not be committed unless a major threat develops at a decisive point. It is a result of the unusual tension prevailing in a pocket that purely local emergenices are often exaggerated and may lead to urgent calls for assistance. Frequently, such local crises subside before long, and the situation can be restored without the use of reserves - provided the pocket commander does not permit himself to be needlessly alarmed.

At this point a few words might be added concerning the attitude that must be displayed by the pocket commander and his staff. In the midst of rapidly changing events the command element must be a tower of strength. The troops observe its every action with keen eyes. In this respect even the location of the command post is of particular importance. While it should be centrally located, its proximity to the momentary center of gravity is even more desirable. Never should the operations of an encircled force be conducted by remote control, from a headquarters on the outside. This proved to be an impossibility, both from a practical point of view and because of its disastrous effect upon the morale of the troops. By the same token, no member of the command group must be permitted to leave the pocket by air. Reassuring information, brief orders issued in clear language, and frequent visits by the commander and his staff to critical points along the perimeter will have an immediate beneficial influence upon the morale of the pocket force. At the same time, exaggerated optimism is definitely out of place. The troops want to know the truth and will eventually discover it for themselves. They are certain to lose confidence if they find out that their commenders have been tampering with the facts in an attempt to make the situation look brighter than it actually is. As a rule, the truth told without a show of nervousness cannot fail to have a reassuring effect and might even stir the troops to greater effort.

Arranged in their proper sequence, the tactical measures leading up to the breakout are the following:

a. Emphasis on defense; all weapons committed in support of the fighting along the perimeter.

b. Establishment of clear channels of command.

c. Stabilization of the defense.

d. Reinforcement of the combat element at the expense of the service units.

e. Evacuation of nonessential personnel; destruction of excess equipment.

f. Gradual change of emphasis from the defense to preparations for the breakout attack.

g. Formation of a breakout force.

h. Shortening of the defense perimeter; further strengthening of the sector selected for the breakout.

i. Deceptive maneuvers culminating in a diversionary attack.

j. Breakout.

Section VI.
SUPPLY AND EVACUATION

The supply reserves carried in a pocket should be no more than what the force will presumably need until the day of the breakout. Sizable stores canot be kept; they must either be given away or destroyed, regardless of quality or quantity. In such situations the Germans found it useful to prepare so-called individual supply packages which were composed of all kinds of items for certain units and could be distributed in advance to the points where they would be needed later on. Surplus rations can be issued to the troops for immediate consumption, but if this is done too generously it is likely to decrease their fighting power. The local population will always gratefully accept whatever the troops can spare.

If a pocket force is without adequate supplies and, particularly, if the required fuel and ammunition can only be brought in by air, the escape from encirclement must be accomplished as quickly as possible. Supply by air cannot satisfy all the requirements of an encircled force; it can only remedy some of the most important deficiencies. This fact was demonstrated during the operations described in the preceding chapters and confirmed by the personal experience of the author. It is not likely to change, even if absolute superiority in the air is assured and an adequate number of planes can be assigned to the operation.

One of the most important logistical problems is that of evacuating casualties. Whether or not the wounded are taken along has a profound effect upon the morale of the encircled troops. Any measure from which they might derive the slightest indication that wounded personnel is to be left behind will immediately reduce their fighting spirit, especially if they are facing an enemy like the Russians. In such situations the commanders are under the strongest moral obligation to take the wounded along and must bend every effort to make this possible. German experience has shown that minor casualties can endure transportation over considerable distances on horse-drawn vehicles padded with straw, even in very cold weather and during snowstorms. On such movements the wounded were accompanied by medical officers who administered every possible aid during the frequent halts. The German troops encircled near Kamenets-Podolskly (Ch. 5) regarded their convoy of casualties as their sacred trust and fought all the more stubbornly to protect their wounded comrades. Consequently, it was possible to evacuate nearly all casualties during that operation. In the pocket near Cherkassy (Ch. 4) the situation was less favorable. There, because of the most severe weather conditions and a confused tactical situation, the wounded had to be left behind in the care of doctors and other medical personnel.

Every opportunity should be used to evacuate casualties by air. They must have priority on transport planes returning from a pocket, and this priority must be assured, if necessary, by force of arms. The desperate struggle for space aboard transport planes in the pocket of Stalingrad should serve as a warning for situations of this kind.

Section VII.
RELIEF OPERATIONS

The difficulties encountered by an encircled force may be considerably reduced if strong relief forces are available in the vicinity of the pocket. Even inadequate attempts at relief from the outside are better than none at all. The basis for real success, however, is the employment of experienced troops in the best fighting condition who are not likely to bog down at the half-way mark. The need for relief from the outside depends, of course, on the tactical situation and the physical condition of the encircled force; it is greatest when the troops inside the pocket are battle worn and show signs of weakening; it may appear less urgent in other situations. But wherever friendly troops are surrounded by the enemy, assistance from the outside is desirable and should be provided without delay.

Such relief operations must be planned with the same care that is used in preparing every action of the encircled force. This applies to the selection of the route of advance, the choice of the proper moment for the attack, and the timely allocation of fuel and ammunition. A relief thrust cannot be launched on the spur of the moment, and undue haste will surely result in failure. Tactical preparations must follow the same principles as those for any other type of attack. The necessary strength of the relief force must be determined on the basis of the enemy situation and the distance to the objective. In most cases armor and adequate artillery support will be indispensable. All relief forces must be under one command, even if they consist of units that were originally parts of two separate armies. (Chapter 4)

Preparatory measures in the fields of supply and administration will greatly exceed those that might be taken for an ordinary attack, since the relief force must try to anticipate the needs of the troops breaking out of the pocket. All kinds of supplies, especially stimulants, must be held ready in sufficient quantities; rescue and rehabilitation areas must be prepared; and facilities must be provided that will improve the physical condition and the morale of the pocket force. Among these are troop quarters (heated shelter in winter), bathing facilities, clothing, and arrangements for mail service. These measures play an important part in getting the pocket force back into shape and ready for renewed commitment. Proper care for the wounded must be assured by assembling all available medical personnel and preparing shelter for the pocket casualties. Information as to the number of wounded inside the pocket must be obtained by radio.

The decision as to the time and place for launching the relief attack depends on specific arrangements with the pocket force. Unless a safe wire communication exists, such arrangements can only be made by radio, in which case great care must be taken to maintain secrecy. The distance to the pocket may be so great as to require the use of special types of radio equipment. In such situations the Germans used their so-called Dezimetergeraet, a microwave radio set operating on frequencies between 500 and 600 megacycles.

If at all possible, the relief attack must be launched on a broad front. A single thrust confined to a narrow frontage has little chance of success and is justified only if insufficient forces are available. (Ch. 2) The relief force, in this case, will have its long flanks dangerously exposed and will hardly be able to reach its objective. If such an emergency method must be used, the operation should be carried out at night.

The conduct of the relief operation must be marked by a high degree of flexibility. Frequently a prearranged plan must be discarded or modified because of unexpected enemy action, particularly if such action is directed against the troops attempting to escape from the pocket. The joint effort of the two converging elements must be geared to the needs of the encircled units who are always fighting under less favorable circumstances than the relief force. The latter must be able to react with swift and effective countermeasures to unforeseen changes in the situation.

The battle west of Cherkassy (Ch. 4) clearly demonstrated what difficulties can be encountered in a relief operation. There, all efforts were frustrated by a combination of unfortunate circumstances. The sudden start of the muddy season had rendered the terrain virtually impassable. Relief forces approaching from the south were whittled down in numerous local engagements before they could be assembled for the main attack. Complicated channels of command and diverging directions of attack further added to the confusion. Certainly, flexibility was lacking in the conduct of the relief operation from the west. The breakout, to be sure, did not proceed entirely according to plan, as the majority of the troops emerging from the pocket missed their direction. Even then they followed a line of advance only a few miles south from the one that had been agreed upon. Because of this minor change, the relief force proved unable to link up with the pocket forces at the point where they had actually pierced the ring of encirclement.

Section VIII.
THE BREAKOUT

Once the pocket force has begun its break-through in the direction of friendly lines, it must apply the same tactical principles and will be subject to the same contingencies as in any other type of attack. A particular difficulty lies in co-ordinating this effort with that of the relief force, for the purpose of accomplishing a junction of the two converging spearheads as soon as possible. German experiences vary as to what would be the most desirable attack formation for a breakout. Since the answer to this question depends largely on the local situation, no definite rules can be offered. In any event it is advisable to adopt a mixed formation composed of motorized and nonmotorized units supported by tanks and all weapons suitable for the attack. Armored units must be held with close rein so as to prevent them front outrunning the infantry. They should only be permitted to advance by bounds, with some of the armor held back. This is a necessary precaution to prevent deep thrusts by individual armored units that can be of no advantage to the progress of the main force. Specific orders must be issued both for the timely integration of all remaining elements to be withdrawn from the defensive sectors and for the conduct of rear guard action to cover the breakout attack.

A major crisis during the breakout will arise as soon as the original plan, for some reason, can no longer be followed and improvisation must take its place. As a rule this will be the result of some unforeseen enemy action. With troops that are severely overtaxed by heavy fighting in the pocket such crises may easily lead to panic. The call "every man for himself" is the signal for general disorder marked by useless attempts of individual soldiers to make their way back to friendly lines. This can only be prevented by firm leadership and strict control, and by taking advance measures that will anticipate such emergencies, as for instance by keeping a mobile reserve, composed of armor and antitank weapons, that can be employed with a high degree of flexibility. Even a few tanks committed at the right moment can serve as a very effective means to overcome a local crisis.

The capabilities of the troops must be carefully weighed and are the basis for the timing of the entire operation. If the troops are battle weary and if the breakout is expected to involve long and heavy fighting, the operation must be conducted in several phases to provide rest between periods of movement or combat. For reasons of security, especially in the case of small pockets, all movements should be carried out during the night. Control of the troops is greatly facilitated if the fighting can be confined to the daytime.

If a breakout must be executed without simultaneous relief from the outside, a new position should be selected in which the liberated pocket force might be able to rally and to face the pursuing enemy; in most instances that will be no more than a line designated on the map where the troops are to be reorganized after their successful escape from encirclement.

Section IX.
SUMMARY

The lessons learned by the Germans during World War II on the relative value of pockets left behind the enemy lines might be summarized as follows:

a. As a method of defensive combat designed to tie down substantial enemy forces, the deliberate stand of an encircled force rarely achieves the desired result.

b. The deliberate creation of a pocket and the insistence on its continued defense can only be justified if the surrounded force consists of experienced and well-disciplined troops who are able to cope with the unusual difficulties involved in this kind of fighting. Otherwise the price will be excessive since the encircled troops are usually lost and even those who manage to escape are certain to remain unfit for combat for a long time.

c. Whenever friendly forces are cut off and surrounded by the enemy, steps must be taken without delay to assure their liberation. The senior commander of the encircled units must be immediately authorized to force a breakout. It is even better to issue a standing order at the beginning of hostilities that would make it mandatory for the commander of an encircled force to break out as soon as possible. Only then can there be any hope of saving the surrounded troops without suffering excessive losses. The German High Command during World War II greatly overestimated the defensive value of such pockets. Orders for a breakout from encirclement were issued either much too late or not at all. This turned out to be a grave tactical error which could not fail to have a disastrous effect upon the entire conduct of operations on the Russian front.

AIR SUPPORT OF ENCIRCLED FORCES

Section I.
GENERAL PRINCIPLES

The air support available to an encircled force will usually determine the feasibility of a breakout and the manner in which it must be executed. As a rule, it will depend on the availability of air cover whether marches and combat actions should take place in the daytime or during the hours of darkness when so many additional risks and difficulties are involved. Since a breakout on a large scale will necessarily include actions that can only be carried out in the daytime, such as frontal attacks over difficult terrain or assaults against well-defended enemy positions, a strong concentration of air power, at least during these phases, is indispensable for the success of the entire operation. In an extensive theater of war, where the air force has to accomplish many diversified missions against widely separated targets, there is always the danger of a dissipation of air strength. It will therefore be the responsibility of the top-level air force command to create in time the tactical and technical prerequisites for temporary mass employment of air power at points of main effort. This is accomplished by establishing and maintaining adequate ground installations in all crucial areas so that the rapid diversion of adjacent air force units (at least for one day's operations) will not present serious difficulties.

How many air force units are required to support an encircled force must be determined on the basis of known enemy strength, the size and vulnerability of the pocket, and its distance from the nearest friendly lines. How much air support can be provided will depend essentially upon the capacity of the airfields, the supply situation, and the intensity of combat on other sectors. The air strength actually needed in such situations can hardly be overestimated. It has to make up for the critical deficiencies that always aggravate the situation in a pocket (lack of artillery ammunition, heavy losses of weapons and tanks, etc.), and to bolster the morale of the encircled troops during their difficult struggle. In addition, since the immediate vicinity of a pocket is usually the scene of large enemy concentrations, the supporting air units will find numerous opportunities to weaken the forces of the enemy. Here, even more than in most other situations, an adequate reserve of air strength should be available, specifically for the following reasons:

a. The defense of a pocket often takes an unexpected turn and may require the rapid commitment of additional air support that can only be provided if ample reserves are available for instant use.

b. The possibility of heavy aircraft losses must be taken into account, particularly as a result of enemy bombing attacks on friendly airfields.

c. The most serious crisis in a breakout may suddenly arise at a late stage of the operation. This will automatically increase the need for immediate air protection, and without adequate reserves such additional air support will not be available at the decisive moment.

d. Entire air force units may suddenly he grounded because of unfavorable weather and terrain conditions such as dense fog or deeply mired airstrips.

Long-range weather forecasts covering a wide area should be made available to the command of the ground forces. Such data can be of the greatest importance in selecting the most favorable time for a breakout, especially if they include an accurate forecast of bad weather periods during which the enemy air force will be unable to operate. Even local and temporary weather conditions can have a direct bearing on tactical decisions. It is conceivable that an encircled force might take advantage of temporary weather disturbances over enemy air bases, which may have the effect of grounding the bulk of the enemy's local air support, while more favorable weather conditions exist behind friendly lines, permitting one's own air units to carry out their missions.

The command over all air force units in an area where ground troops are encircled by the enemy must be in the hands of one air force commander, who should also have tactical control over air formations from adjacent sectors whenever they are committed in support of the encircled force. In addition, all antiaircraft units in the area must be under his command. [Ed.: It should be remembered that in the German organization most antiaircraft units were part of the Luftwaffe.] In the case of an encirclement on a large scale with adequate airstrips and supply facilities existing inside the pocket, it is advisable to appoint a special air force commander for the pocket area, who should be located in the immediate vicinity of the pocket command post. This air force officer should receive his orders from the air force commander responsible for the entire area.

Section II.
PREPARATORY MEASURES

All preparations for air support must be carried out as inconspicuously as possible. Great care must be taken to conceal the intentions of the pocket force and, specifically, to avoid offering any clues as to the time and place of the impending attack. Air supply operations should be initiated at the earliest possible moment, to assure that the ammunition and fuel requirements of the troops for the days of the breakout can be adequately covered. With few exceptions supply by air is indispensable for the success of a pocket force attempting to break through the enemy ring of encirclement. Yet, under the most favorable circumstances supply by air remains an extremely uneconomical measure. Therefore, when encirclement appears inevitable, every possible effort should be made in advance to build up an adequate supply reserve, at least of heavy and bulky items; even after the encirclement has become a fact, this might still be done by a strongly armed supply convoy forcing its way into the pocket.

If a force is compelled by specific orders to submit to encirclement by the enemy, it should seek to make its stand in an area that contains at least one usable airfield. Type and condition of the terrain may render it extremely difficult to accomplish the construction of new airstrips with the limited manpower available. At least one and if possible two or more airfields for the use of supply planes - preferably with cargo gliders in tow - should be in operation as soon as possible. In this instance the ground troops must provide the necessary manpower for grading operations. In some situations it may be imperative to accomplish a widening of the pocket by local attacks, in order to capture a suitable airfield or to place an existing field beyond the range of enemy artillery.

For night operations, which as a rule cannot be avoided, each airfield must have a radio beacon, a light beacon, and an adequate supply of signal flares. All airfields inside a pocket must be under the command of forceful officers supported by experienced personnel, a sizeable number of technicians, and an adequate labor force for the unloading, stacking, and rapid distribution of supplies.

In pockets where suitable airfields do not exist from the outset and cannot be constructed, supply by air is limited to the use of cargo gliders. Although the volume of supplies, in this case, will be considerably smaller, the facilities on the ground, except for the length of airstrips, will have to be virtually the same as described above.

Dropping supplies in aerial delivery containers is an extremely wasteful procedure. Losses from drifting or from breakage upon impact range up to 60 percent; they may be as high as 90 percent if the containers are dropped into the rubble of a destroyed town. Yet, in the case of very small pockets, this may be the only possibility for supplying the surrounded force by air. In that event, the dropping point must be fixed by specific arrangements with the encircled troops since the enemy will make every effort to mislead the approaching planes and cause them to drop their loads over enemy-held territory.

Section III.
AIR RECONNAISSANCE

Air reconnaissance units must provide the pocket commander promptly with the essential information on which he is to base his decisions as to time and place of the breakout and his specific plans for the conduct of the entire operation. The missions to be accomplished by air reconnaissance include the following:

a. Gathering information about enemy dispositions, so as to determine in what area around the pocket the enemy is weakest and where a break-through would have the best chance of success.

b. Furnishing specific information about enemy units located in the prospective breakout area, and indicating targets for counterbattery and air attacks.

c. Detecting enemy reserves and preparations on the flanks of the prospective zone of attack and opposite the rear of the pocket.

d. Providing aerial photographs and photo maps of the prospective break-through area, showing traffic arteries, bridges, and major terrain obstacles, and determining whether or not the terrain is suitable for armored combat.

e. Spotting airstrips (by using aerial photography), which might exist in the path of the planned attack, that could be used for supply by air during the breakout.

Section IV.
FIGHTER AVIATION

If the encircled ground troops are in the possession of adequate facilities and supplies, a considerable advantage can be gained by having part of the fighter force operate from airfields inside the pocket or at least use these fields as advance airstrips for daylight operations. The greater the distance of the pocket area from the main air bases, the greater will be the importance of such measures for the maintenance of the pocket.

As the enemy can be expected to commit strong air units in his major attempt to annihilate the encircled troops - especially if he recognizes their preparations for a breakout - friendly fighter forces eventually have the opportunity of attacking enemy air formations that are confined to a small area, and of shooting down a relatively large number of enemy aircraft.

Section V.
CLOSE SUPPORT OF GROUND ACTIONS

The employment of fighter-bombers (Schlachtflieger) has particular significance in the defense of a pocket where, as a rule, there is a shortage of artillery ammunition and an increased need for concealment and for saving the strength of the encircled troops. Close tactical air support is especially needed during the regrouping of the pocket force just before the breakout. At such time, close-support aviation may have to assume the role and perform the missions of the artillery. To avoid a dissipation of strength, the effort of fighterbombers must be concentrated on a few target areas of major importance. At the same time, great care must be taken against revealing the intentions of the encircled ground troops. The strength and conduct of fighter-bomber units committed immediately before the breakout, for instance, should be largely the same as on preceding days. The targets selected should not permit any conclusions as to the actual direction of the impending attack. If it is necessary to neutralize certain areas in the path of the breakout, this must be done either sufficiently in advance or as soon as the attack on the ground has begun. In addition to providing direct support for the attacking breakout force, fighter-bombers are also employed to prevent the enemy from bringing up reserves and from regrouping his forces for the purpose of blocking the break-through attempt.

As a rule - chiefly for reasons of supply - close-support aircraft must operate from bases outside the pocket. Bombs and other appropriate ammunition that may be available at airstrips within the encirclement should be saved for a maximum air effort on the day of the breakout. Since positions along the perimeter are usually within close range of the enemy and difficult to identify from the air, the greatest caution must be used in the briefing of air crews operating over the area. This applies particularly when long-range aircraft from adjacent combat sectors are employed, a procedure which could otherwise lead to serious losses among friendly ground troops. Such aircraft should first be transferred to airfields close to the area of commitment where the crews can be properly briefed and quickly apprised of local changes in the situation.

Section VI.
EMPLOYMENT OF ANTIAIRCRAFT UNITS

Conspicuous changes in the disposition of antiaircraft units before the breakout may provide the enemy with definite clues as to the intentions of the encircled force. Antiaircraft guns and other tell-tale antiaircraft equipment should therefore be left in their positions (or replaced by dummy installations) until the very day of the breakout. Antiaircraft supply and service elements must be regrouped at an earlier stage, but without attracting undue attention. Similarly, the antiaircraft protection for the ground troops during their assembly before the breakout must be so arranged as to produce the least possible change in the existing pattern of antiaircraft positions. At the same time, an ostentatious concentration of antiaircraft units or dummy positions in an area unrelated to the main effort might conceivably be used as a means to deceive the enemy.

If ammunition reserves are available, which must be left behind, or if the breakout force is without adequate artillery support, it may be advisable to employ some antiaircraft units in direct support of the attack on the ground. These units should be moved during the night before the breakout to double-purpose positions from which they can participate in the initial phase of the operation by delivering direct fire on important ground targets in addition to providing antiaircraft protection.

The general regrouping of antiaircraft units before the breakout should take place as late as possible and with a view to protecting leading ground elements, flank units, artillery positions, and critical points such as bridges and defiles. At this stage it is usually impossible to avoid stripping the remaining ground units and installations of their antiaircraft defenses. Success in carrying out these measures depends in most cases on the degree of mobility retained by the antiaircraft units.

In all these preparations it is essential to keep in mind that the main objectives in the employment of antiaircraft units are protection against low-level enemy air raids and against all air attacks that cannot be warded off by friendly fighter forces. Particularly when the protection offered by fighter aviation is inadequate, the greatest care must be used in co-ordinating the efforts of antiaircraft and fighter units.

For the breakout phase specific plans should be made to

regulate the forward displacement of antiaircraft units and their priority of movement during the advance, provided it is at all possible to anticipate the various moves that might become necessary.

Section VII.
EVACUATION BY AIR

Detailed arrangements must be made by the air force to use supply aircraft returning from the pocket for the evacuation of wounded, of surplus personnel and equipment, and to assist the ground command in carrying out other evacuation measures (to include, in some cases, the removal of industrial equipment). The Army, on the other hand, is responsible for providing adequate medical facilities at the air bases to which the wounded are evacuated. Since casualties must be expected to occur at a high rate during certain phases of the operation, it will be necessary to take care of large numbers of wounded in the shortest possible time.

Section VIII.
AIR SUPPORT DURING THE BREAKOUT

In view of the great difficulties normally encountered during a breakout, the ground troops need protection against persistent attack from the air, as well as continuous tactical air support. Both are indispensable for the success of the entire operation. This is particularly true for the most critical phases of the breakout which occur, first, during the initial attack; second, when the enemy commits his reserves against the flanks and rear of the pocket force; and, finally, when he attempts to overtake and block the troops withdrawing from the pocket. During these phases the air force commander must concentrate all available air units and exert steadily mounting pressure at the critical points. In the intervals between these main efforts he has the missions of preventing interruptions in the advance on the ground, and of keeping his flying units in the highest possible state of readiness. It is, of course, impossible to devise a standing operating procedure for air support during a breakout, since no two situations are alike. Nevertheless, the following basic principles should be kept in mind.

During the initial phase all available air units should be committed in direct support of the leading ground elements. Air attacks on ground targets, beginning with a strong opening blow and continued in successive waves, must be closely co-ordinated with the fire plan of the artillery. The targets of fighter-bombers comprise objectives that cannot be observed from the ground (enemy artillery positions, assembly areas, tactical reserves); also enemy positions offering particularly strong resistance, enemy movements approaching the combat area, and hostile elements threatening the flanks of the advancing spearheads. Standby reserves of fighter-bombers, circling some distance away or, better still, at considerable altitude above the combat area, must be employed to eliminate any reviving enemy resistance and to reduce newly identified enemy strong points. Their presence in the air will greatly strengthen the morale of the attacking ground troops. Experience shows, moreover, that as these planes appear over the battlefield, enemy batteries will cease firing, to avoid being identified from the air. At the same time, low-flying aircraft will often draw fire from hitherto unidentified enemy positions which are thereby exposed to artillery action. Another practicable measure may be the placing of small smoke screens to blind enemy artillery observation.

To avoid hitting friendly ground troops, bombers should operate in the depth of the zone of advance against enemy artillery positions, assembly areas, and similar objectives. They might also be employed to lay large smoke screens, specifically to eliminate enemy observation from high ground off the flanks or from dominating terrain ahead of the advancing troops.

Important objectives in the area of penetration should be reduced before the breakout by thorough bombing attacks, so as to lighten the task of the ground troops during the initial phase of the operation. This cannot be done, however, if such attacks are likely to reveal the plans of the breakout force. Nor does this rule apply to enemy command posts; these must be attacked at the most opportune moment, immediately after the breakout, when the resulting confusion among the enemy of fees the greatest advantage to the attacking force.

The regrouping of enemy units, which, according to German experiences in Russia, might take place between six and ten hours after a breakout has begun, must be recognized and reported by friendly reconnaissance aviation as quickly as possible. From that time on, the enemy should be kept under constant air observation.

In breakout operations of long duration the available fighter forces are usually unable to provide effective air cover at all times. In that event, their efforts must be concentrated on supporting those phases of the breakout which, in terms of terrain and enemy resistance, are expected to involve the greatest difficulties and the highest degree of exposure to enemy air attack. Between these periods of maximum air effort - which must be used to full advantage by the ground troops - it will often be necessary to restrict the employment of fighter aircraft, chiefly because of logistical limitations such as insufficient ammunition and fuel supply. Nevertheless, an adequate fighter reserve must always be ready for immediate take-off in order to defend the advancing ground troops against unexpectedly strong enemy air attacks. The more obscure the enemy air situation, the greater must be the strength of the fighter force held in reserve.

The air support for a relief force that is advancing in the direction of a pocket must, as a rule, be kept to a minimum, in order to assign the strongest possible air cover to the troops that are emerging from enemy encirclement. The forces approaching from the main front line are usually in a much better position to compensate for this deficiency by increased use of artillery and antiaircraft weapons. In such situations, the supporting fire from friendly aircraft must be carefully regulated to avoid inflicting casualties among the advancing ground troops, especially just before the link-up of the two converging forces. Even after the junction has been effected, the former pocket force might require special air protection, at least while its reorganization and rehabilitation are being accomplished.

THE GERMAN CROSSING OF THE DNIEPER IN THE KREMENCHUG AREA (KIEV OPERATION)

Tactical and Technical Trends, No. 7, Sept. 10, 1942

INTRODUCTION

1. GERMAN FAILURE BEFORE MOSCOW AND KIEV, AND PLANS FOR KIEV ENCIRCLEMENT.

August 1941 saw the German Center Group of Armies under von Bock halted in front of Moscow, and the South Group of Armies under von Rundstedt halted in front of Kiev (see map at page 112). There was now no chance for a quick seizure of the capital and a drive by armored spearheads to other strategically important parts of the country as had been the case in France. Plans were shifted to achieve a gigantic double encirclement, which would aim at the capture of the great Ukranian city of Kiev and the destruction of Budenny's armies. The salient between the Desna and the Dnieper, with Kiev at its apex, was to be cut off in a wedge-and-trap operation. The holding attack would be made by the forces which were already in position in front of Kiev. The northern wedge of the encirclement maneuver would have to be driven across the Desna northwest of Konotov, and the southern wedge across the Dnieper below Kremenchug. As preliminaries to the main operation, Uman to the south of the proposed salient and Gomel to the north would have to be taken in order that German troops might advance to the Desna and the Dnieper.

2. IN THE SOUTH - THE UMAN OPERATION.

While the Sixth Army under von Reichenau was halted in front of Kiev, the German armies in the south had been moving forward in conjunction with Hungarian and Rumanian troops. Von Stuelpnegel's Seventeenth Army and von Kleist's First Panzer Army crossed the Bug west of Uman. They helped von Schobert (who had crossed the Bug further south) in the encirclement of Uman and then occupied the right bank of the Dnieper River.

3. IN THE NORTH - THE GOMEL OPERATION.

Von Bock kept up the feint of striking toward Moscow, but shifted to the south the Second Panzer Army of Guderian and the Second Army of von Weichs. These armies encircled Gomel, which fell on August 19, and moved toward their new assembly areas. Guderian reached the Desna near Novogorod on August 30 and immediately established a bridgehead on the south bank. The advance of the von Weichs and Guderian armies toward the Desna also relieved Russian pressure on German forces (von Reichenau's army) west of Kiev.

4. THE SITUATION.

Thus, toward the end of August 1941, the situation was as follows: in front of Kiev the strong army of von Reichenau was in position to launch a holding attack; the von Weichs and Guderian armies some 125 miles to the northeast, and the von Stuelpnegel and von Kleist armies some 190 miles to the southeast, were the potential wedges for encirclement of the Kiev area.

But the maneuver could not be begun, much less completed, until a German bridgehead was established east of the Dnieper. The crossing of this broad and deep river, the third largest in Europe, would have to be attempted in the vicinity of Kremenchug. The operation was entrusted to the Seventeenth Army under von Stuelpnegel, but, according to German custom, the specially created task force was composed of units deemed to be best qualified, irrespective of the command to which they belonged.

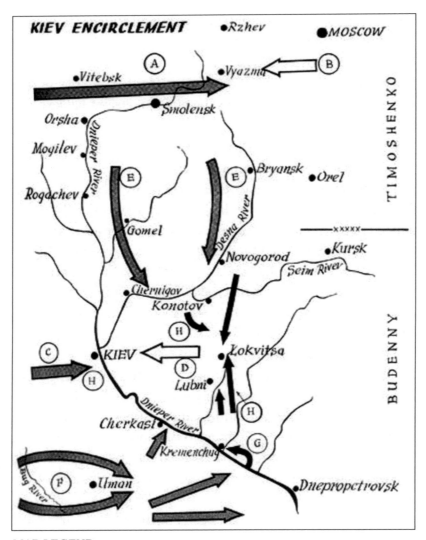

KIEV ENCIRCLEMENT

MAP LEGEND

(A) Von Bock's drive toward Moscow halted by Timoshenko's Group of
    Armies. (B)

(C) Von Rundstedt's drive toward Kiev halted by Budenny's Group of
    Armies. (D)

(E) The von Weichs and Guderian Armies (von Bock Group) advance to the
    Desna.

(F) The von Stuelpnegel, von Kleist, and von Schobert armies (von
    Rundstedt Group) advance to the Dnieper.

(G) The initial crossing of the Dnieper.

(H) The "wedge and trap" encirclement of the Kiev salient.

THE OPERATION

5. SELECTION OF A CROSSING POINT.

The general considerations which influenced the German choice of a point for this difficult operation can be seen by reference to the map.

The area between Kiev and Kremenchug was in every way ill-adapted to crossing operations. From Kiev to Cherkasi, the eastern bank is swampy, and roads would permit the Russians to move troops and supplies easily to a threatened area. Furthermore, a wedge driven across in this area would fail to secure the maximum strategic effect, in that fewer Russian forces would be cut off in the resulting pocket. Between Cherkasi and Kremenchug a crossing is almost impossible; the Dnieper wanders in numerous channels, much of the terrain is marshy, and a tributary (the Tyasmin) parallels the Dnieper on the south.

The area chosen for the crossing, about 25 miles southeast of Kremenchug, possesses several obvious advantages. The Dnieper flows in a single channel, 1,200 yards wide; there are no tributary streams; and the banks are free from swamps. Moreover, in this area the railroads and roads favored the Germans rather than the Russians. On the German side of the river, the Dnieper valley road would be useful at all stages of the operations; on the Russian side, there are no roads to bring reinforcements close to the point of crossing.

A particular feature of the terrain helped the Germans concentrate for attack at this point. The area southwest included a watershed ridge running perpendicular to the river. This ridge was wooded and had sandy soil. The Germans could bring men and supplies by road and rail to a point 30 or 35 miles from the crossing point and advance under cover of the woods, over what was in effect a natural highway almost to the river. The absence of roads would not prevent armored and supply vehicles from negotiating this route.

On the Russian side, the terrain was adapted to exploitation of a successful crossing. Once a bridgehead was established, the Vorskla River would protect it on the right flank, while on the left no natural barrier impeded a German advance toward Kremenchug. North of Kremenchug, the terrain is ideal for a maneuver of envelopment by armored forces. A watershed ridge gave a good route for advance northward by armored units, regardless of damage done to highways or railroads. Each flank of this route was protected by a swampy river.

6. PREPARATION.

Very little information is available on the German preparations for this crossing. In view of its difficulty, and of the importance attached to this operation in the strategy of the campaign, there can be little doubt that a task force was prepared for this assignment according to the usual German principles. These may be summarized as follows:

a. A commander for the task force is selected and given sole responsibility for the operation.

b. He is given troops and materiel according to his estimate of requirements. (This would include, in an operation of this sort, all types of infantry and artillery units, a heavy air component, and important pioneer and transport units.)

c. The commander organizes and trains the units for the specific task assigned. If possible, this is done on terrain similar to that of the proposed operation. The object of this training is to develop a combat team thoroughly rehearsed in all stages of the assignment.

Preparation for the Dnieper crossing involved concentration of considerable supplies of weapons and other necessary materiel. This concentration had to be made as close as possible to the place of projected crossing.

The most serious logistical problem was that of bringing up boats and bridging materiel. German accounts state that hundreds of assault boats were used on the Dnieper River. These boats apparently were of two types--one capable of carrying from 4 to 6 men, and one capable of carrying 10 to 16 men. Both were driven by outboard motors. It is not known how many of these boats were used in the operation, but if "hundreds" were used the problem of transporting and concealing them was an operation of considerable magnitude. Equally difficult was the problem of concealing sufficient pontons and platforms for the construction of a 1,200-foot bridge. Apparently there were enough trees on the sandy ridge to afford cover, yet not so many as to block the movement of wheeled or tracked vehicles.

In this wooded area, camouflage by tree limbs was easy, effective, and much used, as is shown by German photographs. German camouflage emphasizes the value of dummy positions which cause the enemy to waste his ammunition and reveal his position, and which divert suspicion from important concealed installations or supplies. It is quite likely that such positions, with indications of boats and bridging equipment, were constructed at other points on the Dnieper in order to deceive the Russian observers as to the area chosen for the initial crossing.

Concentrations at secondary points along the Dnieper were apparently not so well guarded from Russian air observation. These other concentrations were made partly to divert suspicion from the preparations for the initial crossing, and partly to have heavy weapons and supplies ready for later crossings which would follow after the success of the initial operation.

7. THE JUMP-OFF.

By the end of August, the subordinate commanders charged with execution of the preliminary operations were able to report to the task force commander that they were ready.

At dawn on the morning of August 31, German planes took possession of the sky in the Kremenchug area. German artillery threw a heavy barrage across the river against the Russian lines. At the same moment, hundreds of assault boats were taken from their hiding places and carried down the gently sloping sandy banks to the shallow water at the edge of the Dnieper. The boats, which were designed for this particular type of operation, were probably similar to those which crossed the Rhine in somewhat less than a minute in the Maginot operation (June 1940). No reports have been seen on the time required for the storm boats to cross the Dnieper, but their attainable speed is variously given as 30 to 40 miles per hour.

The boats were not beached at the eastern bank but returned at once for further loads. The speed of the turn-around is to be noted; it is said that the men jumped from the boats as they turned without coming to a complete stop. The small boats carried about 4 men, and the larger boats (judging from pictures) seem to have carried 10 to 12 men. The carrying of less than the maximum loads may have been designed to permit a speedier crossing.

The Germans report that the Russians, taken by surprise, nevertheless immediately organized a determined resistance. Since the steersmen of the German boats stood up, many were killed by the Russian machine-gun fire, which was withheld until the boats were near the shore, but in each instance another soldier took the helm. Preparations had been made for plugging bullet holes immediately, and many boats that received hits were thus enabled to continue across the river. German photographs show spouts of water in the Dnieper caused by Russian artillery shells, and also show sand clouds produced by Russian shells bursting only a few yards from German concentrations on the eastern side. Russian resistance cost the Germans many assault troops, but not enough to endanger the success of the operation.

8. FORMATION OF A BRIDGEHEAD.

As soon as the German assault troops reached the far bank, they immediately began to overcome enemy resistance. The boats crossed the river again and again. The special river-crossing units were followed by more assault troops and by pioneers, and then by the infantry. By noon, enough troops had been ferried over to make the Germans feel that their position was secure. During the afternoon they transported more infantry and further organized their bridgehead. All these operations were continuously reconnoitered and protected by units of the German air arm.

The passage of troops and materiel was now increased by the use of additional, more vulnerable transport. Inflated rubber boats were used for ferrying more men--some 10 to a boat--and ammunition. Large rubber rafts were loaded with heavy infantry weapons, especially antitank guns. These rafts were towed to the eastern side of the river by motor boats. The Germans also prepared ferries consisting of pontons lashed together to support a platform on which heavy guns were towed across the river to be used in neutralizing and capturing the field fortifications of the Russians.

In the meantime the troops which had been transported earlier in the day advanced and took the sand dunes and low hills beyond the opposite shore. The enemy line of artillery observation was thus in German hands. Many troops were now on the Russian side of the river and much materiel had been transported. Since the area was not occupied in force by the Russians, and possessed neither roads or railroads, there was no possibility of an immediate heavy Russian counterattack. Thus, in a single day, a strong German bridgehead had been established. Since they had been carefully rehearsed by specially trained troops, the crossing operations were carried out successfully without great losses.

9. CONSTRUCTION OF THE BRIDGE.

Transport by storm boats, inflated rubber boats, and pontons had been effective, but loading and unloading was necessarily slow. The bridge was needed and, with air superiority in the area and artillery already in place on the Russian side of the river, the Germans did not hesitate to proceed with its construction. This was accomplished in a single night (August 31-September 1), and the next day supplies and troops were pouring across the bridge.

It seems certain that the bridging equipment used in the crossing below Kremenchug was of the type which the Germans refer to as "bridge-gear B": equipment tried out in Poland, perfected, and used for the crossing of the Rhine in the Maginot operation in France.

The basic unit in the construction of a German military bridge is the half–ponton. This is built of metal except for strips of wood on the gunwales. It is 25 feet long, 6.3 feet broad, and 3.3 feet deep. The weight is not known. Half-pontons are used in constructing 4-ton and 8-ton ferries, and sections of 8-ton bridges. Two half-pontons locked stern to stern form a full-ponton. The full-pontons are used in constructing 8-ton and 16-ton ferries and sections of 16-ton bridges. As soon as the pontons are in the water by the shore, the Germans construct platforms on them.

The maneuvering of the bridge section or the ferrying of a ponton-supported raft is accomplished by rowing, by the use of storm boats, by the use of "M" boats (a powerful light motor boat of 100 h.p.), or by the use of outboard motors on the pontons themselves.

German bridging equipment includes prefabricated metal material for building piers at the shore. However, such piers were not needed at Kremenchug. Photographs show that the bank was well drained and sloping, and ramps could easily be used to connect the shore with the ponton-supported bridge.

10. ENLARGEMENT OF THE BRIDGEHEAD.

By the end of August 31, the Russians realized that a major threat had developed. Russian planes made repeated but unsuccessful efforts to destroy the bridge, and also attacked the points of German advance. Hastily assembled Russian reserves made heavy counterattacks with tanks. The Germans, however, maintained their bridgehead, and extended it upstream to threaten the Russian position at Kremenchug.

11. ADDITIONAL BRIDGES AND BRIDGEHEADS.

The Germans gradually enlarged their tactical bridgehead on the east bank of the Dnieper into a strategic bridgehead. Land operations to the northwest reduced enemy resistance 15 miles upstream, at another area free from swampy banks and multiple channels. To gain another route across the river, a second bridge was built at this point, apparently during the night of September 2-3. German reinforcements poured across the new bridge, only 10 miles below Kremenchug. Under their flank attack and a frontal attack from the west, Kremenchug fell on September 8, and the Germans had secured the controlling center of a road and railroad net.

Whether or not the Russians had destroyed existing bridges is not clear. In any case, the Germans felt the need of better transportation across the Dnieper at Kremenchug, and decided to move to that point the bridge which had been constructed 10 miles downstream. The sections were detached and towed upstream during a single night, in a rainstorm, and the bridge was rebuilt at a place where it could serve the Kremenchug road net.

Meanwhile, the Germans had established other bridgeheads across the Dnieper further down the river. These bridgeheads doubtless had the double purpose of paving the way for further operations in the Dnieper Valley and of preventing the reinforcement of Russian troops further north.

12. THE PINCER MOVEMENT BEGINS.

With the eastern bank of the Dnieper at Kremenchug in their possession, and a strong bridgehead established, the Germans had accomplished the most difficult part of the large-scale pincer movement which was to isolate Kiev and destroy a considerable portion of Budenny's armies. The way was now clear for the southern wedge to move. With the First Panzer Army on the right and the Seventeenth Army on the left, the Germans advanced northward along the strategic ridge of high ground from Kremenchug toward Lubni and Lokvitsa, their flanks protected by marshy tributaries of the Dnieper. Meanwhile, from the Desna, the Second Panzer Army moved southward protecting the advance of the Second Army. At Lokvitsa and at Lubni the armored spearheads which had crossed the Dnieper met those which had crossed the Desna, to complete a gigantic double encirclement. The Russians of the Kiev salient were in a trap. The Sixth Army joined the Second and the Seventeenth in the annihilation and capture of Russian forces, while the two Panzer armies protected the operation and moved toward their next objectives. This successful wedge-and-trap maneuver had been made possible by the river crossing at Kremenchug.

13. SUMMARY AND CONCLUSION.

Air superiority is absolutely essential to the success of an operation such as the initial German crossing of the Dnieper below Kremenchug. Airplanes were used in the initial phases for reconnaissance, and to deny reconnaissance to the Russians. Combat aviation guarded the sky above the bridge. Bombardment aviation was doubtless used to harass and neutralize the Russian lines as German troops moved across the newly constructed bridge.

The German success in the Kremenchug operation especially in the initial stages, owed much to surprise, which they achieved by the secrecy of preparations, by deception, and by very rapid execution.

Deception was achieved by obvious preparations for a river crossing at other points in order to draw the defending forces out of position. The incomplete evidence suggests that either actual attempts or feints at crossings may have been made at points other than the one described above. An attempt at Dnepropetrovsk, of uncertain date, is known to have been repulsed.

Speed of execution aided the Germans enormously. By the end of the the first day (August 31), the Russians knew that the operation was of major importance, but the speed with which the Germans built the bridge and moved their forces across the river enabled them to establish a large bridgehead, and prepare to extend it, before adequate Russian forces could be brought up.

In river crossings the Germans send over antitank guns very early in the operation in order to neutralize local tank attacks. Infantry supporting weapons (75-mm and 150-mm howitzers of the infantry regiment) are also ferried over early to support the operation of enlarging the bridgehead.

In the Kremenchug operation, the construction of the first bridge did not commence until after the assaulting formations on the far bank had captured the line of artillery observation; even then the construction was carried out under cover of darkness. Normally, in crossing smaller streams, the bridge-building operations start much sooner, in some cases before the site is clear of small-arms fire. When speed of execution is being employed to achieve surprise, as is often the case with armored forces, much time can be saved by an earlier start even though a few casualties must be accepted. The over-all gain justified those losses.

The German forces employed in the difficult initial crossing of the Dnieper below Kremenchug attribute their success to the secrecy of their preparation, thus exploiting the principle of surprise to the maximum; to good staff work in the careful tactical and technical preparation; and, finally, to boldness and skill in the execution of the plans.

A GERMAN SPEARHEAD IN THE KIEV OPERATION*

Tactical and Technical Trends, No. 11, Nov. 5, 1942

THE ADVANCE OF THE SIXTH ARMY
GENERAL VON REICHENAU'S ARMY.

Among the German forces which crossed the Russian frontier on June 22, 1941, was the Sixth Army, under the command of Field Marshal General von Reichenau. It appears that this army, on the eve of the campaign, was concentrated in German-held Poland in the Biala-Chelm sector immediately west of the Bug River (the Russo-German boundary under the agreement of August 21, 1939). The Sixth Army held the northern flank of the German South Group of Armies under Field Marshal General von Rundstedt. The Sixth Army included motorized infantry and panzer divisions, the Adolph Hitler Regiment (an S.S. unit), and foot infantry divisions, with necessary auxiliary services of all types, and had the support of aviation. "Panzer and motorized infantry divisions, as well as an S.S. unit" are listed by a German source as forming a part of the narrow penetration wedge which was to follow a panzer division spearhead.

In front of Von Reichenau's army was the Russian Fifth Army, which was a part of the Russian South Group of Armies under Marshal Budenny. The order of battle of the Russian Fifth Army is not known.

The German Sixth Army had on its right (southern) flank, the First Panzer Army of General von Kleist, while south of von Kleist was the Seventeenth Army of General von Stuelpnagel.

*This paper is based chiefly on five articles published in the October 16, 23, 30, November 6 and 13, 1941, issues of the Illustrierte Beobachter. The source is believed to be reliable, but details in regard to the order of battle of the various task forces and in regard to the chronology of operations are unfortunately lacking.

These two armies later became the southern arm of the great Kiev encirclement. Further south, von Rundstedt's forces included Hungarian and Rumanian as well as German troops.

North of von Reichenau was the Center Group of Armies under General von Bock. No army of the Center Group maintained ground contact with von Reichenau after the jump-off from concentration areas; ground liaison between the two armies was prevented by the impassable Pripet marshes. East of the marshes, in the Dnieper Valley, the Second Army under von Weichs and the Second Panzer Army of Guderian later established contact with von Reichenau and became the northern arm in the Kiev encirclement.

THE PRIPET OR PINSK MARSHES AND THE ROUTES TO KIEV.

The great marshes of Western Russia are variously called Pripet, after the river which runs through but does not effectively drain them, and Pinsk, for the largest city included in their vast expanse. The term "vast" is not an exaggeration, for the marshes extend from Brest-Litovsk on the German-Russian border eastward to and beyond the Dnieper, a distance of more than 300 miles, and stretch from north to south more than 150 miles.

The marshes had a marked influence on German strategy. Such roads and railroads as existed in them were not first-class. Moreover, a demolition which would be merely a nuisance on dry land would be disastrous in a region where any detour from a road-bed meant hopeless bogging down. Consequently, the marshes could not be effectively penetrated, and were thus a natural boundary between the two groups of armies.

From his concentration area, von Reichenau had to advance toward Kiev along the southern edge of the marshes. The axis of his advance was determined by the disposition of highways and railroads.

At Kowel, the railroad line from Biala and Brest-Litovsk joined the line from Chelm and Luboml. East of Kowel, the

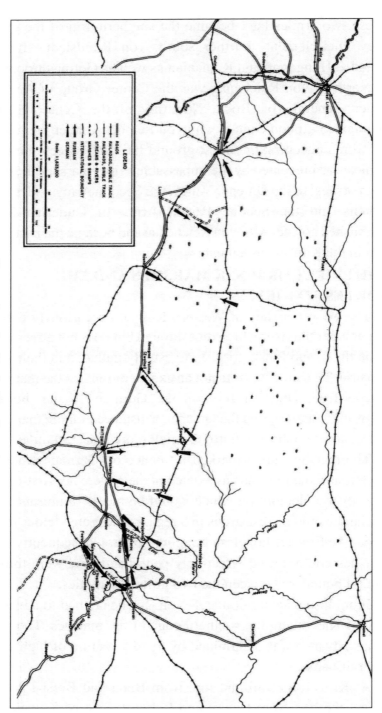

German Spearhead in the Kiev Operation

single line led to Kiev through the southern part of the marshes, across numerous tributaries of the Pripet River. From three of the villages on this railroad, branch lines ran north or northwest toward the Pripet River or the Dnieper (see map). This road and its branches were single-track, and the gauge was different from that of German railroads.

As with the railroads, a highway from Brest-Litovsk and a highway from Luboml met at Kowel, east of which a great highway led to Kiev. This highway was of asphalt and had four traffic lanes from the old Polish-Russian border to Kiev (according to some accounts, all the way from the new German-Russian border to Kiev). This road, which was south of and approximately parallel to the Kowel-Kiev railroad, led through well-drained country and cut across the Pripet tributaries in their upper courses.

VON REICHENAU ADVANCES AND BUDENNY RETREATS.

Because of the difficulties inherent in the use of the Russian railroads, the Germans generally chose the highways for their spearheads in Russia - in this instance, the excellent Kiev highway.

The men and materiel of von Reichenau's Sixth Army had apparently been concentrated as close as possible to the border, along all-weather roads. Some of the first units to enter Russia crossed the frontier near Brest-Litovsk and advanced along the highway from Brest-Litovsk to Kowel. Others, entering further south, advanced along the highway from Luboml toward Kowel. Like the other leading units, which literally rolled into Russia on the morning of June 22, 1941, the forward units of von Reichenau's army again used the spearhead tactics which had been so successfully employed in France and moved forward with great speed, protected by superior air strength. As the Germans advanced, the Russians retreated at an average rate of some 15 miles a day.

To the German commanders, as to observers outside the battle area, the parallel with the campaign in France must have appeared striking. In each case, large areas of important territory were promptly occupied by the Germans.

The Russian withdrawal, however, was not due entirely to weakness. Beyond question, the Russians knew that the Germans had massed great quantities of men and materiel along good highways, just across the Bug. Uncertain exactly when and exactly where these massed Nazi resources would be used, the Russians apparently held their forward positions with delaying forces only and elected to make their main defensive stand many miles to the east. In this way, the Russian commanders were able to learn the direction and strength of the German thrusts before committing the Russian reserves. Even in retreating, they could learn something of German tactics. Finally, when the main engagement would take place, German lines of communication would be long and Russian lines short. These considerations, as well as the strength of the Nazi military machine, probably played a part in the rapid Russian retreat before the German armies in the 1941 campaign. Nor was the German advance made without cost. Battered vehicles abandoned by the road, dead horses, and destroyed villages told of the fury of the Russian rearguard action.

FIGHTING BETWEEN A HIGHWAY AND A RAILROAD.

Since von Kleist was on his right, von Reichenau appears to have had no difficulty on that flank as his spearhead advanced.

On the left (northern) flank, the situation was different. There was no ground contact with the nearest army of the Center Group; this army, in fact, was miles away, north of the Pripet marshes. Moreover, the Russians were in these marshes in considerable force and at once began to harass von Reichenau's left flank. Accurate and heavy Russian artillery barrages came down unexpectedly on German transport.

In spite of this harassment by Russian artillery, von

Reichenau's forward troops continued to move ahead. The area taken by the spearhead troops extended not more than 2 or 3 miles on each side of the highway.

The situation on the marsh flank could not, however, be ignored. Resistance to the Russians was left to foot-infantry troops armed with the necessary heavy weapons and artillery. At every crossroad or junction, a task force had to be constituted to cope with a Russian attack which, if neglected, might threaten the flank. A German commentator, irked by the cost of the operations, stated that a full-scale battle had to be fought for each miserable village, which was worthless in the first instance and rubble when taken.

In the battles between the troops on the highway and those on the railroads, the Germans had the advantage. They were able to move forward more troops and material on the four-lane highway than the Russians could bring up on the single-track railroad, and a Russian retreat was forced. In no case, however, was the bulk of the Russians cut off. When outgunned by superior German artillery and in danger of being flanked by the advance on the highway, the Russian troops retreated along their railroad line to the next vantage-point and again harassed the German advance.

Shortly after the campaign began, the Germans were at Kowel, the junction of the railroad line which the Russians had determined to hold and the highway on which the Germans had determined to advance. After overcoming strong Russian resistance at Kowel, the Germans again moved forward, and took in turn Luck, Rowne, Zwaihel. Soon they were at Zhitomir, an important junction some 75 miles from Kiev.

After crossing several minor streams, their forward elements reached the heights west of the Irpen River. From the summit of this high ground they could see the spires of Kiev. They were 5 miles from the outskirts and 12 miles from the heart of the city. In 20 days they had come 312 miles. With Kiev in sight, an armored division hurried down the four-lane highway toward a wooden bridge over the Irpen.

CHECK OF THE SPEARHEAD AT THE IRPEN RIVER

THE GERMAN SPEARHEAD IS HALTED.

Despite the unexpected and strong Russian assaults which had harassed their advance and were still continuing against their left flank well to the rear, the Germans claim they were confident on July 12 as they started down the western (left) bank of the north-flowing Irpen. Suddenly, in front of them, the wooden bridge of the great four-lane highway was blown out by Soviet troops. Germans often make light of Russian demolitions, but this one they conceded to be perfect. There was nothing left of the bridge, and the steep west banks were under Russian fire. The armored spearheads could not cross the Irpen, and had to retreat up the hill. The delay was annoying, but (according to German sources) it did not shake the confidence of men who had advanced 312 miles in 20 days.

For 20 days they had averaged 15 miles a day; in the next 2 months, however, they were not to move a yard!

The first difficulty was the terrain. Directly in front of the Germans was the Irpen River, a natural bastion of Kiev. Here in its middle course the Irpen had dry banks, but the channel was unfordable. There were many wooded areas on the slopes, particularly on the Russian-held eastern slope, and Russian troops in these woods commanded every yard of open space between the heights on the western bank and the river. Most of the cultivated land was in tall grain, under cover of which the Germans apparently constructed field fortifications. Suburban houses, which offered many opportunities for concealment, dotted both slopes, particularly the Russian-held eastern slope. The four-lane highway cut across the Irpen and ran straight up the hill through a wood toward Kiev, but the bridge was destroyed and every foot of the roadway was under Russian fire.

The Irpen position, moreover, could not be flanked by the German advance units which were halted there. To the north near the mouth of the Irpen, the terrain was swampy, and the Russians held the rail-line in menacing strength. To the south, the upper Irpen, which widened at places into lakes, was an obstacle; and across the divide between the Irpen and the Dnieper, the Weta and the Strugna Creeks were as well defended as the Irpen.

After von Reichenau's leading elements had been halted on the west bank of the Irpen, he immediately devoted himself to a three-fold task: the consolidation of the Irpen position; the elimination of the Russian artillery which was still pounding his supply line and interfering with the bulk of the Sixth Army's movements to its new concentration area east of Zhitomir; and the protection of the Irpen position by operations on the Weta and the Strugna. The accomplishment of these tasks would have the dual result of preventing a successful Russian counterthrust and of establishing the Sixth Army in positions from which, under more favorable circumstances, a further advance might be made.

THE HALTED GERMANS DIG IN AND RECONNOITER.

Von Reichenau's forward units were much over-extended. According to German claims, these units were some 125 miles ahead of the foot-infantry divisions of their army and now had to devote themselves to holding on until the infantry divisions could come forward.

A headquarters for the defending German troops was apparently established in the little village of Milaja, just west of the Irpen, and the main body of the forward troops occupied two shallow ravines more or less parallel with the river. Fox holes were dug at once to give shelter to the troops, who were tired by their rapid advance. Construction was carried out under extreme difficulties. Any movement beyond cover brought a storm of

Russian artillery fire. Russian aviators flew over the German-held houses on the west bank every 2 hours at a height stated by the Germans to be only 35 to 50 feet, dropping 5-pound bombs and machine-gunning the German positions.

There is no reference in available sources to German air reconnaissance over the Irpen position, but such reconnaissance was routine in similar situations and doubtless took place here. Ground reconnaissance was constant. From hidden positions just east of the village of Milaja, officers with camouflaged BC scopes searched the eastern banks of the Irpen. Soon a bunker was discovered. Some hours later a second bunker was detected, and finally the general course of a line of bunkers. Further observation with field glasses led to the discovery of field positions and to the conjecture that there was a tank-trap ditch behind a stockade-type fence. Numerous trucks full of men and materiel were seen to turn off into the woods on both sides of the main highway from Kiev. The Russians were evidently strengthening their already well-defended position.

THE RUSSIANS COUNTERATTACK.

In a few days the Adolph Hitler Regiment took over the position from the spearhead troops, and was later relieved by infantry at dawn on a date unknown but shortly after July 20.

But the Russian reconnaissance and intelligence had been effective. The Russians had learned precisely what was happening on the German side of the river and during the relief of units launched a strong artillery attack. During the afternoon, Russian combat patrols crossed the river on footbridges. Even though the slope on the German side of the river was level and open in comparison with the slope on the other side, Soviet advanced units, under cover of their artillery, succeeded in hiding themselves in small hollows and depressions.

At nightfall, a German battalion was ordered to regain the lost ground. On a front which extended about a mile and a half north and 2 miles south of the highway, the Germans attacked along a line about 500 yards west of and parallel to the Irpen. Under the cover afforded by fields of tall grain, they used machine guns, rifles, and hand grenades against the newly-won Russian positions under fire, however, from Russian mortars.

After a conflict which lasted about an hour and was especially violent along the highway near the blown-up bridge, the Russians were pushed back across the Irpen. The large searchlights, which the Soviets had camouflaged in the treetops, began to flare across the German-held west bank, sweeping the grain fields, and the Germans did not attempt to pursue the retreating Russians across the river. The infantrymen sought out their old fox holes east of Milaja, and an hour before dawn set up their machine guns again in the positions they had occupied before the Russians crossed the river.

THE SIXTH ARMY CONCENTRATES BEFORE KIEV.

Meanwhile, screened by the troops who had repulsed the Russian counterattack on the Irpen, the rearward combat units of von Reichenau's Army continued to move forward rapidly to positions east of Zhitomir.

The one road to Kiev had to be used by almost the entire Sixth Army; it was therefore imperative that any possible jamming and confusion be avoided. Rather than depend entirely upon guides and messengers, the Germans made great use of directional signs. At each junction there were many road markers bearing unit insignia. The signs were especially elaborate at Kotscherowo, where units turned off to protect the southern flank of the Irpen position, and at the junction south of Makarov, where units turned off to secure the northern flank. With these route markers as guides, motor vehicles left the highways without a halt for task missions against the Russian railroad positions or to move into concentration areas. Serials were formed, according to the speed of vehicles or the time a small unit was ready for moving, and the markers with division insignia were relied on to bring the subordinate units together

131

again.

Provision had to be made for servicing and supplying advanced units, and one lane (at least between Zhitomir and Kiev) was designated for west-bound traffic, with three lanes for eastward movement of men and materiel. Over the west-bound traffic lane, transport elements of the forward units went to Zhitomir each night on missions of servicing and supply.

To sum up, the Germans, in the days following July 13, made use of the great highway to strengthen their position on the Irpen, and bring forward troops in great quantities. Some of these relieved the soldiers on the Irpen. Some were thrown off on the left flank to continue the fight for the railroad. Some moved to the South to prevent the Irpen position from being outflanked. Most of them, however, were brought just east of Zhitomir into a staging area which was almost as large as the original concentration area between Biala and Chelm on the west bank of the Bug. Supplies were also brought forward in large quantities. From this new concentration area, troops and supplies were in a position to be moved at the commander's will as operations developed.

OPERATIONS ON THE LEFT FLANK OF THE SIXTH ARMY
THE RUSSIANS CONTINUE TO THREATEN THE GERMAN LEFT FLANK.

While von Reichenau in the days following July 13 was strengthening his position on the Irpen and was bringing forward the bulk of the Sixth Army into its new concentration area east of Zhitomir, Russian artillery was still active on his north (left) flank. The Russians on the railroad had apparently not retreated further eastward than Korosten, and Russian artillery was now dangerously near the new concentration area east of Zhitomir. Accordingly, von Reichenau determined to secure at any cost his exposed left flank, and launched a vigorous assault on the

Russian position at Korosten. The railway junction here was defended by the Russians with bitter determination, and it fell into German hands only after hard fighting; again, the Russians retreated northwest and east along the railroad lines.

THE BATTLE FOR ANDREJEVKA.

By July 23, the Germans had mopped up Korosten and other neighborhoods to the east, and now determined to take Andrejevka. Many details in regard to the struggle for this village are available and are believed to be typical.

For the Andrejevka engagement, German forward units apparently left the Zhitomir-Kiev highway at the junction near Makarov. During the night of July 22-23, several artillery battalions and a smoke battalion moved up under cover of darkness, and took their positions less than three-quarters of a mile from the infantry front line. At 0430, light and heavy field howitzers, 100-mm guns and 180-mm mortars opened fire against the Soviet field fortifications which German observers had detected on the southern edge of Andrejevka. At the same time, German smoke shells fell among the Russian field positions and spread a thick veil of smoke just in front of the village.

The heavy fire preparation, the laying of the smoke screen, and the beginning of the infantry advance had been coordinated. The Russians were blinded; neither their forward infantrymen nor their observers in observation posts could see more than five or six yards through the thick smoke. Unobserved, the German infantrymen left their positions of readiness and rushed across the open terrain toward Andrejevka, whole infantry companies reaching the edge of the village with hardly the loss of a man. The Russians were unable to check the German advance with their heavy weapons, because their firing was based on data obtained before the laying of the smoke screen.

The smoke screen had been launched under ideal weather conditions and remained for a long time.

As soon as the Soviet observers could see through the gradually disappearing smoke, they directed fire against the German attacking infantry. However, the German forward artillery observers quickly informed their batteries of the location of the Soviet artillery and heavy weapons positions. These positions were at once shelled heavily, and soon became silent.

The German infantrymen then entered Andrejevka, which consisted of many field positions, all excellently camouflaged and all liberally provided with machine guns and mortars. Houses and barns had been equipped for defense. The Russian positions were in many cases connected by cleverly arranged trench systems.

THE THREAT TO THE LEFT FLANK IS REMOVED.

The engagement at Andrejevka was basically a struggle for the Korosten-Kiev railway line, which passed a mile or two to the north. With the German capture of this village, following the capture of Korosten and Malin, this vital railroad, except for a short suburban portion near Kiev, was in German hands. The Russians who had threatened von Reichenau's left flank withdrew now to assist in the defense of Kiev. No information is available as to their line of retreat; but most of them probably fell back along the railroad to the strongly held position east of the Irpen. The new Russian front line north of the Zhitomir-Kiev highway became something like the top half of the letter "C".

Overcoming the Russian resistance along the railroad reduced the threat of a Russian flank attack from the north. Few roads and railways led through the Pripet marshes toward the new German positions, and the Germans instead of the Russians were now aided by the fact that a slight demolition could render a whole area impassable.

Von Reichenau had not only secured his left flank; he was also getting into position to make contact (previously denied him by the Pripet marshes) with von Bock, whose Second Army and Second Armored Army were soon to move down from the north.

OPERATIONS ON THE RIGHT OF THE SIXTH ARMY

A CORPS MOVES TO SUPPORT THE RIGHT FLANK.

While elements on the northern flank of von Reichenau's army were attacking Russian positions on the railroad north of the Zhitomir-Kiev highway, one of his corps was assigned a mission to the south. The mission of this corps was not only to assist in securing the Irpen position but to put von Reichenau's army into areas from which an assault upon Kiev could be made when the situation permitted.

The German units destined to take part in the large-scale operations south of the Irpen position turned off the main Zhitomir-Kiev highway at Kotscherowo, and proceeded in a southeasterly direction by way of Brusilov to Fastov. German panzer and motorized infantry divisions went first along the paved road, which stopped at Fastov, some 40 miles southwest of Kiev. Beyond Fastov, the troops had to advance toward their new positions along ordinary roads, which had been turned into mud by a three-day rain.

On a front of some 12 miles running from southeast to northwest astride the Fastov-Vasilkov-Kiev road, five infantry divisions were moved up to establish prepared assembly areas from which an attack was to be made later against Kiev. Fastov was the center of combat for the entire sector, since it was the only practical road to Vasilkov, the one city of any size between Fastov and Kiev. There were regimental assembly areas on each side of this road.

Two villages, Gelenovka on the left and Marjanovka on the right, flanked the roadway some distance in front of these assembly areas, and as the Germans approached these villages they encountered difficult terrain, for the Strugna had many tributary creeks with steep slopes. The two villages had, moreover, been very heavily fortified by the Russians, and here again, as north of the Zhitomir-Kiev highway, the Germans were compelled to use their heavy weapons and expend themselves in force against unimportant localities which the Russians had transformed into fortresses.

THE GERMANS USE DIVE BOMBERS AND TANKS IN CAPTURING THE VILLAGE OF GELENOVKA.

The German heavy artillery had been moved into position, apparently south of Fastov, and by July 30 von Reichenau felt that his southern corps was ready to launch an attack toward Kiev. The attack was made at 0400 on a 12-mile front. Artillery concentrations fell on Gelenovka and Marjanovka--and at the same instant similarly heavy Russian artillery attacks were directed upon the German positions. The Germans learned later from prisoners that the Russians had, by an unusual coincidence, made their plans for an attack upon the German positions at this same hour.

Under the cover of fire by their artillery, German infantry troops moved into positions of readiness at the bottom of the small valley in front of Gelenovka. During this movement, they were under fire from Russian artillery.

Either by previous plan or because of the unexpectedly heavy Russian artillery fire, the Germans sent in eight dive bombers at 0530. The German and the Russian artillery fire ceased as the planes appeared. These dive bombers released their bombs at an altitude of about 450 feet. A decrease in Russian fire indicated that Soviet observation posts and guns had been hit by the bombs.

The advancing German infantry, however, had to cross broad fields of ripe grain before arriving at the edge of the village. In accordance with their customary tactics, the Soviets had taken advantage of the cover afforded by the grain and, digging deeply into the black soil, had constructed an elaborate system of field positions to protect the village. Russian machine-gun fire from flanking positions, as well as carelessly directed German infantry fire, increased the difficulties of the forward German units as they moved through the grain fields. There was heavy hand-to-hand fighting for the Soviet machine-gun and rifle nests. Finally, the leading German units reached the edge of Gelenovka. There again machine guns, rifles, and hand grenades were used on both sides in close combat in front of the village.

In spite of bitter and incessant fighting from 0400, Gelenovka was still held by the Russians shortly before sunset. At this time, German armored assault artillery advanced through lanes among the halted forward elements and charged into the village, firing in every direction from which resistance appeared. Riflemen followed closely and beat down any resistance not broken by the assault artillery. At sunset Gelenovka was finally captured. The exhausted infantry sat at the side of the road amid dead Soviet soldiers, crushed horses, and burned vehicles and watched a stream of Russian prisoners led to the rear.

According to German sources, an equally severe struggle was necessary to secure possession of other villages, including Marjanovka. When Marjanovka was taken, the Germans felt that they had entered the outer protective ring of the positions in front of Kiev.

THE GERMANS ARE STOPPED AT WETA CREEK BY RUSSIAN DEPLOYMENT IN DEPTH.

On July 31, German troops worked forward from Marjanovka toward Vasilkov, the only city on the road to Kiev from the south. German observers with glasses sought for any possible show of hostile resistance in the tall grain. Infantrymen combed the grain fields and the steep slopes of the Strugna tributaries.

The Russians harassed the German advance by artillery fire; however, they evacuated the inhabitants of Vasilkov, and did not defend that city. The Germans entered the town, established headquarters, and dug in around the outskirts to protect the units and supplies which were brought up.

During the forenoon of August 1, the leading German

elements continued beyond Vasilkov in close pursuit of the Russians. After passing through several villages and crossing several swamps, the Germans, encountering increased opposition, approached the Weta, which the Russians had determined to hold. Russian artillery and mortar shelling of the German forward positions was extremely heavy on August 1, 2, and 3.

In front of the Germans and across the Weta, the Russians had constructed a semicircular line of bunkers similar to those further north along the Irpen River. The Germans at once began efforts to force these positions. At dawn on August 3, a young lieutenant succeeded in leading his platoon into the valley through a ravine obscured from the enemy. The platoon crossed the Weta and surprised a hostile security group located behind wire obstructions and an antitank ditch. Although accurate Russian shellfire prevented this platoon from holding its position, the observations reported by the lieutenant formed the basis for his battalion commander's attack. During the evening of August 3, German heavy weapons units, varying from heavy mortars to light field howitzers, completed their movement into positions in front of the Weta bunkers. Fire began at once, and hits were registered on positions located by observers in advance posts.

On August 4 at 0400, German artillery opened a heavy concentration of fire against Russian fortifications in the woods across the Weta. Three Russian bunkers received direct hits. After 45 minutes of continuous firing, there was a lull of five minutes, and at 0450 the German shelling was renewed with increased intensity. Smoke mortars next went into action; their shells exploded in front of and between enemy bunkers, and covered the center of the valley with a smoke cloud. Artillery fire was continued. The commander of a German infantry battalion leaped out of his cover, led his companies down the slope, through the knee-deep Weta, and across a 70-yard open space to a lane cut through the Wire entanglements by the bridgehead platoon. Fortunately for the Germans, the bunker which protected the antitank ditch just beyond the wire had been put out of action by a mortar.

After crossing the antitank ditch, the right flank rifle company encountered another band of wire entanglements. Pioneers rushed to the front and cut a lane, through which a second special group of pioneers moved against the bunker on the right, bursting it open with two concentrated explosive charges. Then the flame throwers squirted their liquid fire into the hatchways, and a black smoke cloud obscured the view for some minutes. The Germans pushed on into the forest and found numerous abandoned field positions dug deeply into the earth. Their artillery fire had destroyed Russian resistance in that particular area. In places, the forest was a jumble of giant craters, broken trees, and torn branches. The air was full of dust mingled with the smell of exploded shells. A rolling barrage of German artillery, directed by observers with the leading elements, lifted just ahead of the Germans advancing through the forest. Finally the Russians were pushed out of their last positions in this area, which was over 100 yards inside the forest and a little more than a mile from the creek.

Simultaneously, other Russian bunker positions were penetrated, not only here, but on the front of the entire corps attacking on the south. The Russian fortifications were arranged in great depth, however, and this corps, while it had scored minor gains, could not effect a break-through.

Under heavy Russian fire the German riflemen lay on either side of the road in deep trenches which protected them from hostile shell splinters. They were surrounded by ankle-deep mud, and stretched pieces of canvas over themselves for shelters. They did not shave or wash for days. The field kitchens were several miles in the rear, and by the time meals could be served the food was cold. But, in spite of difficulties; the Germans held their position in spite of strong Russian counterattacks. They thought, according to their own accounts, that they would reach Kiev in 2 or 3 days. However, they remained in their positions, 12 miles from the heart of the city, and for a number of weeks made no advance against the determined Soviet resistance.

In the meantime the Germans strengthened their positions, turned Vasilkov into a headquarters town, and brought up supplies and reinforcements again by an all-out attack, which made no appreciable headway.

VON REICHENAU'S HALTED ARMY BECOMES THE HOLDING ATTACK OF THE KIEV ENCIRCLEMENT OPERATION

The situation before Kiev was finally resolved in September by events many miles away, both south and north. In the south, von Stuelpnegel had thrown a bridge across the river below Kremenchug, (see Tactical and Technical Trends No. 7 p. 40), and still nearer German forces had established bridgeheads across the Dnieper at Kanev, Rjishchev, and Tripole. Thus the west bank of the lower Dnieper was in German hands.

In the north, von Kleist had crossed the Desna near Novgorod-Seversky. Also, on the northern flank, a German advance to the northeast had forced the Russians out of Garnostaipol and across the Dnieper. The more northern elements of von Reichenau's Army had also established connection with von Weichs's army which had advanced north of the Pripet marshes, and had turned southward and crossed the Desna.

If the Germans had planned to take Kiev by a frontal attack, they had failed. Von Reichenau's army in two months of effort made no appreciable headway on the Irpen and on the Weta. The Germans had, however, dug themselves in so that they could not be easily thrown back. Whether the Germans had planned to take Kiev and had failed, or whether they had planned merely to secure strong positions before that city, they were now ready to become the holding attack in the envelopment which followed.

On September 17 at 0630 von Reichenau, once more began his attack on the Russian positions. As usual, violent artillery bombardment, assisted by dive bombers, paved the way for assaults with mortars, machine guns, hand grenades, and other weapons. The Russians again defended villages so stubbornly that each village outside of Kiev was destroyed. Because of the closing of the trap by armored troops far to the east of Kiev, however, the Russians had to cease their resistance, and withdraw across the Dnieper River. The city was captured by the Germans on September 19. Despite their heroic 10 weeks of resistance to the Germans in front of Kiev, the outflanking operations of von Bock from the north and of von Rundstedt from the south had forced the Kiev defenders into a disastrous position. The Russian soldiers who had fought so valiantly were withdrawn across the Dnieper, but were not able to escape from the trap which closed around at least four and possibly five of Budenny's armies.

THE GERMAN ADVANCE FROM THE NORTH - KIEV OPERATION

Tactical and Technical Trends,
No. 16, Jan. 14, 1943

INTRODUCTION

Upon entering Russia on June 22, 1941, the German Center Group of Armies under Marshal von Bock had little difficulty in effecting a double encirclement of the cities of Bialystock and Minsk. After this victory, von Bock again pushed his group of armies eastward and effected the encirclement of Smolensk, a strategically important city known as the "western gate of Moscow". Despite the fact that the capture of Smolensk (August 6) had proved costly, von Bock again thrust forward--this time apparently in an attempt to encircle Viazma. The fighting was bitter. The German Second Panzer Army was cut off by the Russians and was rescued only by a lavish use of air power. The spearhead of the Center Group of Armies was definitely brought to a halt by Marshal Timoshenko before Moscow.

THE KIEV OPERATION

After the failure of the German Center Group of Armies to make further gains toward Moscow, and after the similar failures of the North Group of Armies approaching Leningrad and the South Group before Kiev, the Germans initiated the great double encirclement, which is generally referred to as the Kiev Operation. It is not known whether this operation was envisioned before June 22, or whether it was attempted as the only large operation possible after the failure of the frontal attacks against the three great cities.

In any event, the plan was as follows: Kiev was to be enveloped and as many as possible of Marshall Budenny's armies were to be trapped and destroyed in a gigantic double pincers envelopment, or wedge and trap operation (see map on page 150). The holding attack, and the two southern pincers arms or the southern wedge were to be from the South Group of Armies under Marshal von Rundstedt. Von Reichenau's Sixth Army, which had been halted on the Irpen River west of Kiev, was to launch the holding attack. The Seventeenth Army of von Stuelpnegel and the First Panzer Army of von Kleist were to constitute the two southern pincers arms of the southern wedge. The wedge from the north was to be formed from the Center Group of Armies of Marshal von Bock. The Second Panzer Army under General Guderian and the Second Army under General von Weichs constituted the northern pincers arms. The outer pair of pincers, the two Panzer Armies, was to close about 125 miles east of Kiev.

Of course, no two double pincers or wedge-and-trap (Keil and Kessel) operations are exactly alike, but the Kiev operation may be regarded as typical. The scheme of maneuver was basically the same on both flanks. The outer pincers arm (a panzer army) drove forward to meet the approaching arm. As the armored spearhead moved on, small task forces were thrown off on the outer flank for security, and on the inner flank to drive the Russians toward troops of the inner pincers arm (composed chiefly of infantry divisions) or against natural obstacles, or to envelop them, and, in any case, to destroy them. Simultaneously with the advance of the armored pincers arm, infantry armies broke through to form the inner pincers and devoted themselves primarily to the annihilation of pockets of troops cut off by the outer Panzer pincers arms. To sum up, between the jaws of the closing pincers--in this case two pairs, an outer and an inner-- the enemy is crushed. Or, in the other figure of speech, when the wedges meet, the trap is closed and the enemy is exposed to total annihilation.

TWO "MOSCOW" ARMIES TURN TO THE SOUTH

The southern flank of von Bock's armies extended from the apex of his advance at Roslavl through Rogachev to the Pripet Marshes. On the eastern end of this long flank, Guderian's Second Panzer Army faced to the south and von Weich's Second Army which had advanced in the rear of Guderian's forces, also faced south on the western end of this flank. The mission of both armies was to drive southward, capture the city of Gomel, trap the Russian forces in that area, and seize bridgeheads across the Desna. The Second Panzer Army was to protect the east flank of the southward moving forces from Russian counterattack. The Second Army was to establish contact across the east end of the Pripet Marshes with von Reichenau's Sixth Army, the most northern army of von Rundstedt's South Group of Armies. The German advance was in general over thickly wooded and marshy terrain. Prior to August 12, the Germans were advancing on the entire Russian front.

THE EASTERN ARM OF THE DOUBLE PINCERS IN THE NORTH

At the beginning of the Kiev Operation, the Second Panzer Army was in the vicinity of Roslavl, a railroad junction on the old Post Road which led south from Smolensk. Its main body apparently advanced south from Roslavl, over the only motor road leading in that direction. Soon after the advance in the new direction began, another element moved southwest, probably with the double purpose of cutting Russian supply lines and shielding more closely the Second Army's left flank. Concerning this advance, there are no available details from Russian sources, but German claims, that the Second Panzer Army rolled back the Russians by a flanking movement to the west before reaching the Gomel-Bryansk railroad, would indicate that the Panzer elements left the south road at Mglin and pushed toward Gomel.

The Panzer elements which occupied Chernigov probably left the Post Road further south at Starodub, but some or all of them may have left the Post Road at Mglin and may have turned south from the Mglin-Gomel road.

The Germans state that Unecha was bitterly contested. No further details are available, except that the Second Panzer Army captured the junction and pushed on to the south. Another German source states that on August 17, there was a tank battle about 130 kilometers (80 miles) south of Roslavl. This was probably the fight for the Unecha junction.

Unlike the road followed by the Second Army from Mogilev to Gomel and thence to Kiev, the Second Panzer Army's road via Unecha to Novgorod Syeversk was not a first-class road, and the available German accounts of the fighting deal in large part with bad road conditions brought about by heavy rains. According to a German source, the vehicles literally had to grind their way through deep mud. The ground was so soft, according to this source, that log roads constructed by the Germans were pressed far into the mud and rendered almost useless by the weight of the supply elements of the German columns. Since the season was summer, it appears that the drying-out of roads was rapid; in any event, Novgorod Syeversk on the Desna was reached. Here bridgeheads were at once established south of the Desna, and the Second Panzer Army was rapidly reorganized and made ready for its part in the Kiev encirclement.

THE WESTERN ARM

At the time of its right turn to the south, the Second Army under von Weichs was apparently concentrated about 100 miles west of Roslavl in the Mogilev-Bobruisk area. A part of this army drove south toward Gomel over a first-class road paralleling and east of the Dnieper. As in the case of the advance of the Second Panzer Army, no details are available concerning this drive to the south.

According to German sources, a flank attack was launched on Gomel by troops which advanced via Jlobin (in some accounts south of Jlobin) and struggled through the Pripet Marshes. Because of the difficult terrain and lack of roads, these troops, however, were probably a relatively small part of the Second Army. No road (according to available maps) leads directly from the Bobruisk area to Gomel. Even the roundabout routes were over poor roads. The road from Rogachev to Jlobin was worse than second-class; no road led all the way from Jlobin to Gorval; and the road from Gorval to Gomel was second-class or worse. Thus German troops, by whatever route they approached Gomel from the west, faced bad road conditions.

The Second Army encircled and destroyed pockets of Russians at Rogachev and Jlobin and soon struck at Gomel. Despite a strong Russian counterattack, the maneuver, which was apparently an envelopment, was completely successful. The defenders were trapped and the city fell on August 19. According to a German source, infantry, artillery, and engineers had all played major roles; prisoners numbered 84,000; 144 tanks, 949 guns, 38 airplanes, and 2 armored trains were captured.

It appears that von Reichenau's final campaign for seizing the Brest Litovsk-Kiev railroad was not begun until after the success of the Second Army's drive was indicated. Those Russians on the railroad who could not get back to Kiev tried to escape through the marshes and across the Dnieper to Chernigov, but elements of the Second Panzer Army, which presumably had moved over the Starodub-Chernigov road, were already in that city, and the retreating Russians were trapped. Since Chernigov dominated several routes to the east, its loss was a serious blow to the Russians.

PREPARATIONS ARE COMPLETE

By August 21, the Germans held all territory north of the Desna, and both of the northern pincers arms were ready for the final phase of the operation, the advance southward below the Desna into the Russian-held Kiev salient.

While the Second Army and the Second Panzer Army were crossing the Desna into their newly established bridgeheads, other related events had been occurring. Northwest of Kiev, the holding forces of von Reichenau drew nearer to the city after the defeat of the Russians along the Brest Litovsk-Kiev railroad. Von Reichenau's forces had also approached nearer to Kiev on his south flank and, though unsuccessful in an apparent effort at taking that city, had developed strong bunker lines and other defenses behind which troops had been brought up for the Kiev holding attack. This attack, coordinated with the operations south of the Desna, was now launched. Simultaneously in the south, von Rundstedt's South Group of armies had on August 31 thrown a bridge across the Dnieper River below Kiev at Kremenchug, and had effected crossings at other places. The troops of von Kleist's First Panzer Army became the outer pincers arm and the troops of von Stuelpnegel's Seventeenth Army became the inner pincers arm of the envelopment from the south.

THE SECOND ARMY CROSSES THE DESNA

No details are available in regard to the advance south of the Desna by the German Second Army, but the road-net and the general tactical situation would indicate that some elements drove south by Kozelets toward Kiev and that others, further east, drove toward Priluki. Each of these roads was an admirable route for the Kessel part of the wedge-and-trap (Keil and Kessel) maneuver. The road via Kozelets for miles commanded the double-track Kiev-Moscow railroad, and the junction at Brovari commanded every highway available for a withdrawal from Kiev. The road via Priluki at and south of Piryatin likewise intersected important Russian roads and railroads, and continued southeast of Lubni (see below).

THE SECOND PANZER ARMY CROSSES THE DESNA

The Second Panzer Army crossed the Desna just beyond Novgorod Syeversk, the first large town inside the northern boundary of the Ukraine. The Desna, which is some 655 miles long, is the largest tributary of the Dnieper.

The river was defended by strong and extensive fortifications along the eastern and southern banks. German sources state that the bunker walls here consisted of two timbers, each 12 inches thick, with an intervening space of 24 inches filled with sand.

As the Germans advanced, the service of engineers was constantly needed. The Germans had to repair a damaged bridge across the Desna and had to build a ponton bridge over the Seim.

At Konotop where the railroad from Kiev to Moscow intersected a north-south highway, the Russians resisted stubbornly, for they realized that the loss of Konotop would not only prevent supplies from being sent to the retreating armies in the trap, but would imperil the retreat of these armies from the trap. However, the Germans captured the city and the outer armored pincers arm was free to advance the remainder of the distance across the northern half of the Kiev salient. As the advance elements moved forward, other troops came up and held the town and protected the rear.

After the Germans took Konotop, the Second Panzer Army drove straight across country toward Romni. A very heavy rain began to fall as the leading battalion entered the town. It rained continuously on September 11 and 12, and German armored vehicles had great difficulty moving in the mud. Large towing-machines and caterpillar tractors were the only vehicles which could pull out the heavy trucks loaded with fuel, ammunition, and supplies. At times the supply elements were completely out of contact with the combat elements. Even the engineers, according to the Germans, were powerless because of the mud. Drivers used tree trunks and branches, wire rolls, and wooden fences to make wheels take hold, and yard by yard the vehicles moved forward.

The bad weather did not last long, and the main body of Germans reached Romni. German tanks drove through the town and across the first bridge beyond without much trouble. However, the Russians opened fire on the unarmored vehicles following in the rear. A second bridge, at the exit of the town, was stubbornly defended by snipers with automatic weapons in cleverly built positions along the steep embankment on the far side of the river. German engineers and riflemen finally drove the Russians out of the emplacements by going around and attacking from the rear. Then the armored spearhead moved on towards Lokhvitsa, farther to the south.

As the Germans moved south they met, with ever greater frequency, Russian troops attempting to flee from the trap, the closing of which was by now obvious to the Russian commander. Some Russians escaped, but the rapid closing of the trap caught most of the Kiev defenders inside.

THE NORTHERN WEDGE MEETS THE SOUTHERN

As the Germans approached Lokhvitsa, they captured three bridges but encountered resistance. The Soviet forces made a counterattack supported by antiaircraft guns using direct fire. Some tanks and a truck with quadruple-mounted machine guns attempted to take the bridges from the Germans. These Russian vehicles approached to within 300 yards and then their attack slowed down in the face of the fire of German antitank guns and howitzers. Since they drove back but did not destroy the attacking Russians, the Germans protected their positions by laying mine fields. On Friday, September 12, some of the German armored vehicles entered the town, and on Saturday the 13th, they pushed on to villages only some 25 miles from the northward-moving tanks of the First Panzer Army of General

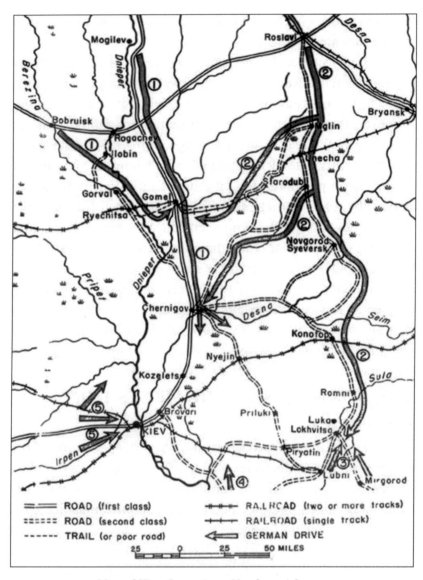

Map of Kiev Operation - Northern Advance

MAP LEGEND:
1. *Approximate routes of the Second Army of von Weichs.*
2. *Approximate routes of the Second Panzer Army of Guderian.*
3. *Spearheads of the First Panzer Army of von Kleist.*
4. *Spearhead of the Seventeenth Army of von Stuelpnegel.*
5. *The holding attack of the Sixth Army of von Reichenau.*

von Kleist.

The closing of the armored pincers was to take place without delay. On Sunday, September 14, a strong reconnaissance element of the Mark Brandenburg Panzer Division from the Berlin area, cut the Kiev-Kharkov railroad, over which supplies were brought for the Soviet armies in this area. This panzer division continued to advance southward. By this time the advance elements of a Panzer division from the Rundstedt South Group of Armies had penetrated as far north as Lubin.

As the northern arm moved south over the last miles, it encountered Russian trucks and horse-drawn wagons. These were dispersed by fire and the advance continued. A German reconnaissance plane was overhead. Radio messages were constant. Shortly after 1430, the valley of the Sula was entered. River crossings were necessary, and dangerous highway defenses were encountered, but the heights at Luka were reached at 1620. Two hours later the advance elements reached a demolished bridge on a small tributary of the Sula. Across the stream was an armored reconnaissance detachment of a Vienna regiment belonging to the First Panzer Army of the South Group of Armies. The armored pincers arms from the north had met the one from the south. The advance continued on to Lubni.

While the advance continued south from Lokhvitsa to Lubni, a spearhead from the South Group of Armies were being driven north from Mirgorod along the highway, to Lokhvitsa. No difficulties were encountered, since elements of the Mark Brandenburg Division were already waiting for the advancing elements of the Vienna Division. The wedge operation was completed.

THE KESSEL

According to German practice, the two outer encircling Panzer arms threw out on their outer flanks enough tank elements to prevent a breakthrough by any Russian forces to the east. Troops of the inner pincers arms were enabled to devote themselves exclusively to entrapping and capturing the Russians. The Second Army elements referred to above .as moving via Kozelets and Priluki had the help of Von Stuelpnegel's Seventeenth Army which moved up from Kremenchug. Crossing the Dnieper at Kiev, von Reichenau's Sixth Army also attacked the Russians who were attempting a withdrawal. Hemmed in on all sides, the Russians were soon defeated. The German mopping-up maneuvers apparently consisted chiefly in minor wedge and trap operations in any area where German forces could either encircle a body of Russians or pin it against a natural obstacle. The Germans pronounced the Kiev operation officially concluded on September 22, and claimed that 665,000 Russians, including four or five of Budenny's armies, were captured.

The figure, however, seems excessively large unless (as is German custom) all able-bodied men in the district were counted as prisoners of war. In fact a German account intimates that women as well as men were counted in the total: "female riflemen.... refused to be regarded as civilians. They were soldiers and could shoot machine guns and pistols like a man. So they had to march with the male prisoners."

CONCLUSIONS

Several conclusions can be drawn from the Kiev encirclement:

(1) A large encirclement operation is more than a simple advance by armored troops. It generally begins by an initial breakthrough toward some definite point, the occupation of which will threaten a vital line of communications.

(2) Secondary pincers movements may be expected at any point as the operation develops.

(3) Emergencies must be met by subordinate commanders on the spot by intelligent action in harmony with the general plan.

(4) Superiority in the air, superior mobility on the ground, and smoothly functioning radio communications are absolutely essential.

(5) Supply and vehicle maintenance agencies must be prepared to cope with unusual and often precarious situations. Security must be carefully planned and vigorously executed.

(6) From German accounts it would appear that Panzer forces often operate with calculated recklessness and without flank protection. These forces in fact operate ahead of the main body, but a study of an operation will usually reveal that the exposed flank of the rapidly moving units is protected by natural obstacles or by adequate forces assigned to this mission, or by both.

(7) An important principle of the successful encirclement is the application of greatly superior combat power at decisive points. The German plan was to immobilize, surround, and annihilate units before they could be thrown into action.

(8) The fundamental steps in the German plan of operations may be summed up as follows: first, to locate the enemy through reconnaissance and espionage; second, to disrupt enemy communications by air power; third, to concentrate decisively superior strength at vital points, with full use of secrecy, deception and speed of execution; fourth, to encircle and annihilate the hostile forces.

TACTICS: SPECIAL OPERATIONS

Handbook on German Military Forces

1. Town and Street Fighting

In attacking a town or village, the Germans employ flanking and encircling tactics. They attempt to cut off water, electricity, gas, and other utilities. While carrying out the flanking maneuver, they pin down the defenders with heavy artillery fire and aerial bombardment. When it is necessary to make a direct assault, the Germans concentrate all available heavy weapons, including artillery and air units, on one target. They favor as targets for their massed fire the forward edges of the community, especially detached groups of buildings and isolated houses. During the fire concentration the infantry assembles and attacks the objective immediately upon termination of artillery fire. Tanks and assault guns accompany the infantry, and with their fire immobilize any new enemy forces which may appear. They also support the infantry in sweeping away barricades, blasting passages through walls, and crushing wire obstacles. Guns and mortars are used against concealed positions, and antitank guns cover side streets against possible flanking operations. Machine guns engage snipers on roofs.

The immediate objective of the Germans is to divide the area occupied by the enemy. These areas then are isolated into as many smaller areas as possible, in order to deny the enemy freedom of movement.

Another form of attack employed by the Germans is to drive through a community and establish good positions beyond the town to block the retreat of the defender. Then they try to annihilate the enemy within the community.

The assaulting troops are divided into a number of columns

and make a series of coordinated parallel attacks. Attacks from opposite directions and conflicting angles are avoided, since they lead to confusion and to firing on friendly troops. The columns are sub-divided into assault and mop-up groups. Assault detachments of engineers, equipped with demolition equipment, flame throwers, and grenades, accompany the infantry. Where possible, the Germans blast holes through the walls of rows of buildings along the route of advance in order to provide the infantry with covered approaches. These passages afford protection for bringing up supplies and evacuating casualties. Houses are cleared of defenders by small-arms fire. Streets are avoided as much as possible by the Germans who infiltrate simultaneously through back yards and over roofs. They attempt to further the advance by seizing high buildings which offer dominating positions and wide fields of fire.

When compelled to advance through streets, the Germans move in two files, one on each side of the thoroughfare. The left side is preferred as it is more advantageous for firing right-handed from doorways. Consideration is given to the problem of fighting against defenders organized not only in depth but in height. Consequently the men receive specific assignments to watch the rooms, the various floors of buildings, and cellar windows. Side streets are immediately blocked, and at night searchlights are kept ready to illuminate roofs.

As soon as a building is occupied, the Germans organize it into a strongpoint. Windows and other openings are converted into loopholes and embrasures. Cellars and attics are occupied first in organizing for defense.

Even buildings which have been completely destroyed are kept under constant observation to prevent their reoccupation by the enemy. From occupied buildings the Germans deliver continuous machine-gun and rifle fire with the object of denying the enemy the opportunity to occupy alternate positions.

Underground corridors and sewers, which provide excellent

cover for defenders, are attacked with determination. When immediate clearance or smoking-out is not possible, the entrances are barricaded, blasted, or guarded.

Aware that their tanks and assault guns are vulnerable to attacks by tank-hunting units, the Germans assign infantry to protect them. Barricades and obstacles are cleared by infantry and engineers. All able-bodied civilians, regardless of danger, are summoned to clear the streets of debris.

When a section of a town is occupied, the Germans close up all side streets leading from the occupied area, block all exits of houses, and then begin a house-to-house search with details assigned to special tasks, such as mopping up roofs, attics, basements, courtyards, and staircases.

2. Attack on Fortified Positions

The Germans realize the difficulty of attacking a strongly fortified enemy position and prepare such an attack well in advance of the actual operation. Before attacking a large and intricately fortified position covering a large area—a classical example was the assault on the Belgian Fortress Eben Emael— the Germans attempt to secure, in addition to information obtained through normal reconnaissance, its exact plan by the employment of agents and fifth columnists. When time permits, they construct a duplicate of the fortification on similar terrain well in the interior of Germany, as they did with Eben Emael. In building such installations for intensive rehearsal training of specially-organized combat teams, the Germans spare neither labor nor expense. These special combat teams usually consist of combat engineers, reinforced by infantry, antitank, and chemical warfare units.

The attack on the fortress usually is preceded by an intensive dive-bomber bombardment and long-range heavy-artillery fire. The purpose of these bombardments is to destroy obstacles and minefields, and to create bomb craters which not only provide cover for assaulting troops but also may be converted into firing positions. Often paratroopers land in close proximity to the fortification just prior to the assault, immediately establishing radio communication with the combat-team headquarters.

The climactic phase of the operation is the assault. Its primary objective is to get the engineers forward to certain selected works. During the approach, and until the engineers reach the fortifications, the artillery delivers fire of maximum intensity. Antitank guns lay direct fire against the embrasures, and chemical-warfare units employ smoke to blind forts and adjacent supporting works. The infantry covers the embrasures with rifle and machine-gun fire and remains in readiness to move forward and consolidate any success the engineers may gain. Engineers crawl forward, utilizing shell holes for cover. They are equipped with hand grenades, blocks of TNT, and submachine guns. Some groups use bangalore torpedoes, some pole-charges, while still others are armed with heavy flame throwers. With TNT and pole charges, they attempt to demolish systematically the weaker works, such as embrasures, ports, turrets, joints, and doors.

3. Combat in Woods

When attacking in woods, the Germans usually divide the area into company sectors. The Germans stress constant reconnaissance to discover the most weakly manned enemy position. This reconnaissance is carried out, even though company strength becomes temporarily reduced. Reconnaissance patrols usually move clockwise from their original position. The company commander reviews the reconnaissance reports in detail with his platoon and section leaders.

The company usually deploys in wedge formation when advancing. In order to achieve surprise, the Germans often leave the roads and advance cross-country.

As soon as the point of the wedge of the company is in sight of the enemy, the Germans creep forward to close-combat range, always keeping contact with adjacent and supporting units. The company then storms the enemy's position, using the greatest possible number of hand grenades, pole charges, and close-combat weapons. The advance elements attempt to break into the hostile position as deeply as possible, the body of the wedge widening the peneration on both sides. The company commander then decides whether to roll up the enemy position on the more important flank or to hold the ground until reinforcements arrive before continuing the attack.

Each platoon details at least one observer, armed with an automatic weapon, to neutralize enemy treetop snipers. The Germans believe that bursts of fire, rather than single shots, are necessary to deal effectively with such snipers.

The Germans consider fighting in wooded areas as the primary task of riflemen and machine gunners, since the employment of heavy-support weapons often is impossible. The Germans occasionally dismount heavy machine guns and use them as light machine guns. Antitank guns of small caliber and light infantry howitzers sometimes are brought forward manually, and when indirect fire is not possible they engage targets directly. Light mortars are employed individually. From Finnish troops, the Germans learned a successful method of using mortars in woods. The mortar observers, accompanied by a telephone operator, move with the advanced element. The line back to the mortar crew is exactly 200 yards long. One man is detailed to see that the line does not get hung on the way and as far as possible runs in a straight line. When the advanced element contacts the enemy, the observer judges the distance from himself to the target and adds the 200 yards to the mortar range. Bracketing of fire for adjustment is considered too dangerous because of the close proximity of friend and foe.

When the Germans leave a woods or have to cross a large clearing within the wooded area, the troops work themselves close to the edge of the woods. Then all the men leave the woods simultaneously, rushing at least 100 yards before seeking cover.

4. Combat in Mountains

a. GENERAL.

The German principles of combat in mountain areas correspond in general to those employed on level terrain. The peculiarities of mountain terrain, such as limited routes, extreme weather conditions, and difficult communications, necessitate additional considerations in the tactics employed. The greatest differences occur in the higher mountains, where the Germans utilize specially trained mountain troops, which include the renowned Tyrolean and Bavarian mountaineers.

The Germans emphasize that all operations will be of longer duration in mountainous country than in lowlands, and therefore make proper allowance for the factors of time and space. For every 330 yards ascent or 550 yards descent they add 1 hour to the time estimate for covering a given distance on the map. Movements, command, and supply in mountain areas represent sources of difficulty, according to the Germans.

b. TACTICAL CHARACTERISTICS OF MOUNTAIN WARFARE.

The Germans divide their units into numerous marching groups, which normally consist of a reinforced infantry company, an artillery battery, and an engineer platoon. In this manner the Germans counteract the danger of ambush, since each group is able to fight independently. The Germans locate their engineer units well forward with the advance guard so that they may assist in road repairs. The Germans realize that small enemy forces can retard the advance of a whole column and therefore they have single guns sited well forward. They also organize stationary and mobile patrols for flank protection.

The skill and leadership of junior commanders are severely tested in mountain warfare, as forces generally are split into small groups, the efficient command of which requires a high standard of training and discipline. Columns often are separated by large areas and impassable country, and since lateral communication is often very difficult, command of deployed units becomes much more complicated than over level terrain.

Normally supplies are organized in two echelons, the mountain and valley echelon.

The Germans make extensive use of high-trajectory weapons in mountain fighting, although antitank guns and heavy machine guns are used for covering road blocks. The effectiveness of the mountain artillery depends on carefully selected observation posts which are in communication with the single gun positions.

Radio is the primary means of communication, since the laying of telephone wire is not considered feasible.

c. MOUNTAIN TACTICS.

Attacks across mountains are made to protect the flanks of the main attack, to work around the enemy rear, or to provide flanking tire for the main attack. The Germans attempt to seize commanding heights and mountain passes.

The Germans select their assembly areas as close to the enemy as possible to make possible a short assault. Supporting weapons are attached to companies, and where feasible, to platoons.

In defense, the Germans organize their advance positions on the forward slope, while the main battle position with heavy-support weapons is located on the reverse slope. The greater part of a unit often is held in reserve. This necessitates the organization of relatively narrow sectors, which, however, results in an organization of ground favorable for counterattacks.

5. Winter Warfare

Many of the techniques of German winter warfare were developed from those of the mountain troops, which were adapted easily to conditions of extreme cold.

Ski patrols are the chief means of reconnaissance in snow-covered terrain. As a rule, the strength of the patrol is a squad, reinforced by infantry soldiers trained as engineers, artillery observers, and a communication detachment. In addition to normal reconnaissance missions, patrols obtain information as to the depth of the snow, load capacity of ice surfaces, and danger of avalanches. These ski patrols normally blaze trails by marking trees or rocks and by erecting poles or flags. Stakes are used to indicate the extremities of roads.

Under winter conditions, German units keep support weapons and artillery well forward while on the march. Their antitank weapons are distributed throughout the entire column. Ski troops are organized to guard the flanks. Sleighs are added for the transport of weapons and supplies.

The Germans assign to trail units the task of cutting tracks for the formations that follow. The strength of the trail unit of a company is one or two squads; that of a battalion up to two platoons. In difficult terrain their strength may be doubled. Trail units are divided into a number of trail detachments consisting of six to ten men, echeloned behind the first of the trail units. The march formation of ski troops is generally single file; usually parallel trails are used to reduce the length of the column.

In winter warfare, attacks with limited objectives are the rule. The Germans attempt wherever possible to combine frontal and flank attacks under conditions of extreme cold and snow. They employ support weapons as far forward as practicable. Attacks often are made by ski troops; because of the difficulty of transporting artillery, ski troops frequently have to dispense with artillery support. For this reason the Germans consider it all the more necessary to concentrate heavy and light infantry weapons at points of main effort and to coordinate high and flat trajectory weapons. When pack howitzers are available, they can be dismantled and brought forward on sledges. Assault guns can effectively support ski troops in snow under 16 inches deep.

They either accompany the attack as far as road conditions allow or move into positions at effective range, not exceeding 3,500 yards, on specially cleared paths away from roads. They occupy their positions just before the attack. As a rule attached assault guns are employed in platoon and company strength; single commitment is avoided. Tank units are attached only in exceptional circumstances.

Organization of a defensive position in deep snow or on frozen ground takes considerable time, for it is necessary to move weapons into position, lay out foot paths and roads, and build strong outposts and strongpoints with all-around defense. Camouflage is particularly stressed under such conditions. Since normal units used as reserves in deep snow have only limited mobility, the Germans employ ski troops for reserves wherever possible. These ski units are used for immediate counterattacks which are directed, where possible, against the flank of the attacking enemy. The Germans also use the ski troops as raiding parties to harass the enemy's front and rear.

6. Partisan Warfare

a. GENERAL.

In order to understand German anti-partisan measures, it is necessary to discuss briefly the characteristics of Allied partisan organizations and their fighting techniques. The following discussion is based entirely on official German sources. The principles involved may be accepted by the Germans and find their way into actual practice in the near future.

b. TASKS OF PARTISAN WARFARE.

The Germans consider that the strategic mission of the Allied partisans was to inflict maximum injury on the German Armies of Occupation. Means employed to accomplish this task were as follows:

- Raids on individual drivers, resting places, troop and supply trains, headquarters, airfields, and ammunition and supply

dumps.
- Demolition of bridges, roads, and railway tracks.
- Destruction of wire communications and railway systems.
- Destruction of industrial installations and crops.
- Terrorization of collaborators.
- Undermining the morale of locally recruited auxiliary troops.

c. ORGANIZATION OF PARTISANS.

(1) **General.** Allied partisan forces were organized partly prior to German occupation and partly during the occupation when dispersed army personnel and civilians rallied around a common leader. The Germans list the following elements as sources for the recruitment of Allied partisan units:
- Remnants of Allied units which escaped destruction during military operations.
- Individual stragglers.
- Smaller units or individual members of Allied forces who infiltrated through the German lines.
- Allied parachutists.
- Escaped prisoners of war.
- Deserters from locally recruited auxiliary services.
- Civilian volunteers.
- Terrorized civilians.
- Women, who may be employed either as combatants or auxiliaries in the supply, medical, or signal services.

(2) **Russian partisan units.** The Germans outline the composition of Russian partisan units as follows:
- Diversion groups of three to ten men.
- Combat units of 75 to 100 men, divided into two or three companies, each of two or three platoons.
- Battalions.
- Regiments, consisting of several battalions.
- Brigades of several hundred men.
- Units of several thousand men, of varying composition and fighting value.

- Divisional headquarters in command of operational groups.
- Corps headquarters controlling a certain number of brigades or regiments.
- Scouting and reconnaissance detachments.
- Higher intelligence headquarters.

In addition the Russians had signal organizations and special formations for demolition works and bridging, mounted detachments, and in some cases even artillery and antitank guns. A special ground organization was set up to serve the air forces which supplied the partisans.

(3) French partisan units. The composition of the French partisan forces, according to the Germans, is:
- The squad consisted of four or five men.
- The platoon consisted of approximately 30 men.
- The company had approximately 100 men.
- A battalion consisted of three or four companies.

(4) Weapons. The weapons of the partisans included rifles, light machine guns, light mortars, pistols, machine pistols, hand grenades, explosives and incendiary material. Battle units also had heavy machine guns, heavy mortars, and guns.

(5) Uniforms. Partisans had no standard uniform. They wore civilian dress and the most diverse uniforms of their own and enemy forces. Stocks of uniforms were maintained by raiding German supply depots.

(6) Camps. The partisans located their camping areas in inaccessible terrain such as dense forests, marshes, wooded mountains, and caves. The camps usually were fortified with field works, dugouts, tree platforms, and minefields. Normally a number of camps were set up in adjacent areas with alternate camp sites prepared. The camps were complete with dumps, slaughtering facilities, bakeries, dressing stations, and weapon repair shops. These camps were well guarded, the personnel of the guard being composed of partisans or of volunteers from nearby communities.

d. PARTISAN TACTICS.

(1) General. Higher headquarters would issue directives of a general nature, and the leader of the smaller detachments would determine the method of execution. In accordance with their strategic function, partisans almost always avoided pitched battles. If trapped and forced to fight, they would follow different courses according to their strength. Large bands would fight it out, whereas smaller units endeavored to disperse by small groups, infiltrating through the lines of the attackers or disguising themselves as harmless and peaceful civilians. Defensively, partisans fought with determination, even ferocity, from behind well fortified and camouflaged positions, allowing the attackers to approach to close range, and then delivering concentrated surprise fire. In Warsaw, Polish partisans fought in building areas for weeks with much skill, inflicting considerable losses on the Germans.

(2) Fighting methods. The partisans carried out guerrilla operations by conducting surprise raids against headquarters, camps, and weapon depots of the occupation army or by ambushing military transportation facilities, columns, or convoys.

When raiding columns, the partisans constructed obstacles along the route and then destroyed the first and last vehicle of the column. Railway trains were destroyed by exploding the roadbed or removing trackage. Troops trying to escape from trucks or trains were taken under fire. Before an attack partisans usually destroyed all telephone communications.

Partisan bands often changed their field of operations in order to carry out a given task, to secure supplies, or to evade discovery and prevent encirclement. Strict discipline on the march was maintained. Marches were generally at night, by routes known only to the local population. Partisan bands have marched 40 to 45 miles daily.

A common ruse was to give the appearance of greater strength by disseminating false information concerning partisan strength and armament. Partisans frequently used military uniforms of the occupation army for purposes of reconnaissance and requisitioning.

For successful operation the partisans needed secret agents who could be found in almost every village. The intelligence service of the partisans, of necessity, employed large numbers of women and children. In addition to collecting information, they were used as messengers between various partisan groups. (Local civilian populations usually were summoned to give assistance to the partisans.)

e. GERMAN ANTI-PARTISAN MEASURES.

(1) General. The Germans divide the measures to be adopted against partisans into offensive action and passive defense measures. Both constitute specialized types of activity, brought about by the particular methods employed by the opponent. Since the partisans are inferior in armament, regular troops are inclined to underrate them and to act without due care and precaution. According to German doctrine, dealing with partisans demands increased vigilance, boldness, and aggressiveness in order to meet their extraordinary cunning and cruelty. In addition, the Germans considered that special training was necessary for their own troops in order to overcome difficult types of terrain such as woods, marshes, mountains, and built-up areas as well as for fighting at night or under winter conditions. Experience taught the Germans that the success of their anti-partisan measures depended on proper coordination between the German Armed Forces, SS, police, and the civil administration, ignoring, when necessary, territorial boundaries.

(2) Offensive action. The Germans centralized the command and control of their anti-partisan measures and made arrangements in regard to the fields of responsibility between the supreme command of the armed forces, the SS Reichsführer and the Chief of Police. While in 1942-1943 the responsibility for the organization and direction of these measures rested with the supreme command in operational areas and with the SS Reichsführer in the so-called Reichskommissariat, the latter, upon acquiring increased powers, assumed complete responsibility.

Subordinate to the SS Reichsführer were the Chief in Command of Anti-partisan Formations (Chef der Bandenkämpfverbande) and the senior SS and police commanders, under whose command Army and Air Force units occasionally are attached.

All German troops and, in emergency, civilian establishments were prepared to engage partisans. The Germans employed the following army units in combat against partisans: divisions, independent task forces, cavalry units, motorized units, armored trains, service troops, emergency units, and locally recruited units. In addition to these organizations, the Germans employed Navy and Air Force units, as well as SS and police formations, including the security service (Sicherheitsdienst) and Secret Field Police (Geheime Feldpolizei).

The Germans emphasized the equipping of their anti-partisan units with easily transportable and quick-firing weapons, such as small arms, machine pistols, automatic rifles, rifles with telescopic sights, light and heavy machine guns, light and medium antitank guns, light infantry guns, light antiaircraft guns, and light flame throwers. Heavier artillery, antitank and antiaircaft guns, tanks, and armored cars, although they effectively strengthened the forces, could not be employed in all situations and terrain.

Clothing and equipage were designed to enable the unit to operate in all types of terrain and under all weather conditions.

The Germans realized the necessity of intensive intelligence work for successful anti-partisan measures. Higher commanders kept situation maps based on information concerning the partisans transmitted by all headquarters and units of the armed forces, and by civilian establishments. Systematic observations were made by security branches, such as the security service, the secret field police, and the military intelligence (Abwehr); information was disseminated and exchanged by adjacent establishments.

To provide all the necessary data for the tactical employment of anti-partisan forces, the Germans conducted intensive reconnaissance preceding their operations. This was carried out by collaborators, by mobile patrols. or by reconnaissance aircraft. Collaborators were the only means of reconnaissance employed when the projected operation had to be kept absolutely secret. The interrogation of prisoners was considered one of the best sources of information. The Germans therefore abandoned their original practice of shooting captured partisans on the spot.

When the Germans had adequate forces available they attempted to encircle and annihilate partisan units. The planning for this operation included the determination of the ground to be encircled, usually limited to the area actually known to be held by partisans. The assembly area was well removed from the areas to be encircled and was occupied in such a manner that the offensive intention was not disclosed. All forces taking part in the operation moved from the assembly area so that they reached the encircling lines at the same time. Lines were chosen which could be defended easily, such as lines of hills or forest paths across the direction of the advance.

The Germans normally kept sufficient local and mobile reserves armed with heavy support weapons. The consolidation of the encircling line was considered decisive for the outcome of the operation, because partisan fighting patrols tested the German lines with the object of breaking out through weak spots. The consolidation of the encircling line followed the usual principles for defense, such as disposing forward battle outposts, drawing up fire plans for light and heavy support weapons, fortifying strongpoints for all-around defense, and keeping mobile reserves in readiness. The precise method by which the encircled partisans were annihilated depended on the forces the Germans had available, on the terrain, and on the reaction of the trapped unit. One method employed was the gradual compressing of the encircled pocket, possible only in restricted areas, because in large areas the encircling forces could not advance at the same rate, thus creating gaps through which partisans could escape. Another method employed was to exert pressure from one side of the pocket while the troops on the opposite side confined themselves to defense. This method was used when the partisans held ground easy to defend, such as a river course, a ridge of hills, or edges of woods. The Germans also utilized powerful wedges and split up the defense pocket into several smaller pockets which were mopped up separately. Another method was to attack from the encircling line by strong assault groups formed from reserves, in cases where battle reconnaissance indicated that the partisans intended to defend their center position.

When time and forces for an encirclement were not available, the Germans attempted to defeat partisan bands by surprise attacks, intending to pursue and wipe out single detached groups. This method proved to be of value where a partisan formation had not been able to consolidate its position. The German actions therefore were dependent on the methods adopted by the partisans. When they committed their forces for battle, the German attack was carried out systematically with concentrated forces and fire. When the partisans attempted to avoid contact, the Germans pursued them frontally, while other units carried out enveloping movements. When the partisan formation dissolved, however, the Germans had to undertake reconnaissance to locate their new assembly area before a new action could begin. The primary target in such actions was the leader of the partisans, and the Germans usually placed a premium on the head of the leader to encourage his capture or death.

The Germans employed large numbers of heavy support weapons, tanks, assault guns, self-propelled antitank guns and heavy howitzers, when fighting the partisans in communities, and concentrated all available heavy weapons against a single objective. The tactics employed followed the German combat methods for street fighting and combat in towns.

The Germans also employed combat patrols against the partisans, copying the latter's methods with the object of harassing the bands and hindering their assembly and supply. Areas which were used regularly by the partisans for food requisitioning, or which they crossed on raids or sabotage expeditions, offered good opportunities for the deployment of German combat patrols. These patrols consisted of hand-picked, tough, well trained "Partisan Hunters" of platoon to company strength. They often wore civilian clothes or partisan uniforms.

(3) Protection measures. Offensive anti-partisan operations were supplemented by vigilant protective measures designed to safeguard troops; road, rail, and waterway communications and traffic; industrial, administrative, and signal installations; and growing crops and forest preserves.

The Germans designated the security of troops as a command responsibility. As a rule the Germans did not billet units of less then company strength in lonely districts. All billets and camps were organized for all-around defense, and all guard rooms were made into strongpoints. Maps showing the local partisan situation were consulted before the march.

To protect railway installations the Germans organized special protection forces whose task included patrolling in addition to the protection of communication centers. Strongpoints were constructed inside all installations and often along the tracks.

The Germans also organized special forces for the protection of roads and waterways. These forces, "Sicherungstruppen", were supplemented by military police detachments on the roads and water police on the waterways.

The ruthless methods employed by the Germans to maintain law and order are too well known to be discussed in this book. From the killing of individual suspects to the wholesale slaughter of whole communities and the burning of villages there is one long line of German atrocities and brutality.

f. GERMAN PREPARATION FOR PARTISAN WARFARE.

Beyond doubt the Germans prepared and are still preparing fanatical members of the National Socialist Party, SS, and armed forces for partisan activities as the territory occupied by the Allies increases. One of Heinrich Himmler's main duties as commander-in-chief of the Home Army is supervising the establishment of partisan organizations and stay-behind agents in areas about to be occupied by the Allies. The Germans have built up large stores of ammunition and supplies, particularly in the mountainous areas of the country, and have established at various localities training centers for future German SS Partisans. Women are included in this training program. As to the methods which the Germans are most likely to employ, no definite information can be revealed at this time. However, it is recommended that a study of the Allied partisan combat methods be made to obtain an approximate conception of possible German partisan activities.

7. Anti-Airborne Operations

The Germans consider the use of mines and wire obstacles particularly effective against enemy airborne operations. They block landing fields and areas where landings might be made with S-mines, stakes, ditches, piled earth, stone, and wood, nondescript vehicles without wheels, and other barricades. They also construct minefields and dummy minefields.

For the protection of important installations against airborne attack, the Germans organize an all-around defense, giving particular attention to covering avenues of approach with machine guns. Observation posts are set up on high points, such as church towers and terrain features to give early warning of hostile landings. Such posts are located also in rear areas, and are especially important in thinly populated localities, since wire communications are particular targets of enemy airborne troops. Special signals by church bells, drums, or bugles are arranged for alarming the German mobile reserve units. These units, specially organized for the task of counteracting enemy airborne invasions and partisan activities usually consist of motorized troops with machine guns and antitank guns mounted on their vehicles. Although the Germans consider it an error to delay in committing these units, they stress that care should be used to avoid enemy deceptive maneuvers such as the dropping of dummy parachutists.

The Germans usually withhold rifle fire until descending parachutists are at close range, using machine-gun fire at greater distance. They believe that fire is most effective immediately upon the landing of the hostile force, before a consolidation of position has been made. Enemy transport planes are considered particularly good targets since they must reduce speed just prior to the jump of the troops.

The Germans appreciate the importance of immediate action against airborne troops and when no alternative is possible they will commit inferior forces to combat the hostile aerial invasion, hoping to delay the attack until reserves can be brought up.

TACTICS: OFFENSIVE

Handbook on German Military Forces

Types of Attack

a. FLANK ATTACK (Flankenangriff).

The Germans consider that the most effective attack is against the enemy's flank. The flank attack develops either from the approach march—sometimes through a turning movement—or from flank marches. It attempts to surprise the enemy and permit him no time for countermeasures. Since mobility and the deception of the enemy at other positions are required, the flank attack is most successfully mounted from a distance; the troop movements necessary for the maneuver can be executed in close proximity to the enemy only with unusually favorable terrain or at night. Attacks are launched on both flanks only when the Germans consider their forces clearly superior.

b. ENVELOPMENT (Umfassungsangriff).

The envelopment is a combination flank-and-frontal attack especially favored by the Germans. The envelopment may be directed on either or both the enemy's flanks, and is accompanied by a simultaneous frontal attack to fix the enemy's forces. The deeper the envelopment goes into the enemy's flanks, the greater becomes the danger of being enveloped oneself. The Germans therefore emphasize the necessity of strong reserves and organization of the enveloping forces in depth. Success of the envelopment depends on the extent to which the enemy is able to dispose his forces in the threatened direction.

c. ENCIRCLEMENT (Einkreisung).

An encirclement, the Germans think, is a particularly decisive form of attack, but usually more difficult to execute than a flank attack or an envelopment. In an encirclement, the enemy is not attacked at all in front, or is attacked in front only by light forces, while the main attacking force passes entirely around him, with the objective of maneuvering him out of position. This requires extreme mobility and deception.

d. FRONTAL ATTACK (Frontalangriff).

The Germans consider the frontal attack the most difficult of execution. It strikes the enemy at his strongest point, and therefore requires superiority of men and materiel. A frontal attack should be made only at a point where the infantry can break through into favorable terrain in the depth of the enemy position. The frontage of the attack should be wider than the actual area (Schwerpunkt) chosen for penetration, in order to tie down the enemy on the flanks of the breakthrough. Adequate reserves must be held ready to counter the employment of the enemy's reserves.

e. WING ATTACK (Flügelangriff).

An attack directed at one or both of the enemy's wings has, the Germans teach, a better chance of success than a central frontal attack, since only a part of the enemy's weapons are faced, and only one flank of the attacking force or forces is exposed to enemy fire. Bending back one wing may give an opportunity for a flank attack, or for a single or double envelopment.

f. PENETRATION (Einbruch) AND BREAKTHROUGH (Durchbruch).

These are not separate forms of attack, but rather the exploitation of a successful attack on the enemy's front, wing, or flank. The penetration destroys the continuity of the hostile front. The broader the penetration, the deeper can the penetration wedge be driven. Strong reserves throw back enemy counterattacks against the flanks of the penetration. German units are trained to exploit a penetration to the maximum so that it may develop into a complete breakthrough before hostile countermeasures can be launched on an effective scale. The deeper the attacker penetrates, the more effectively can he envelop and frustrate the attempts of the enemy to close his front again by withdrawal to the rear. The attacking forces attempt to reduce individual enemy positions by encircling and isolating them. The Germans do not consider a breakthrough successful until they overcome the enemy's artillery positions, which usually is the special task of tanks. Reserve units roll up the enemy's front from the newly created flanks.

The Germans often refer to this maneuver as "Keil and Kessel".

STREET FIGHTING BY PANZER GRENADIERS

Intelligence Bulletin, October 1943

German Panzer Grenadiers (armored infantry) are given extensive training in street fighting. Cooperating with tank units, the Panzer Grenadiers are often employed for the close-in combat that is required when the Germans wish to put an end to all resistance within a town—generally one which has been, or is being, encircled. The following extracts are from a Panzer Grenadier lieutenant's account of such an action. In spite of its Nazi point of view and its heightened style, it is interesting as an illustration of Panzer Grenadier activity. The action the lieutenant describes takes place on the Eastern Front. A well-deployed tank battalion, followed by a Panzer Grenadier company riding in armored personnel carriers, is advancing across the plains of the Ukraine.

A Russian force has been encircled, and the task for today is to drive through the center of the pocket and divide the Russians into still smaller groups, which can be destroyed separately. As yet, no rounds have been fired, but the tanks ahead of us may come upon the hostile force at any moment. The company commander glances at his platoons; they are following in considerable depth and width. The distance between vehicles is at least 50 feet, the radios are set for reception, and everything is in order. It is very hot, and there is a haze.

The men in the tanks ahead can see a village in the distance. According to the map, this should be Krutojarka. Guns can be seen flashing at the edge of the village. The Russian force is engaged. We hear the fire of Russian antitank guns and our own tank cannon, and, in between, the sound of both sides' machine-gun fire. The Panzer Grenadier company commander gives his command by radio. As soon as the grenadiers see Russian soldiers, they are to fire on them directly from the personnel carriers, or else dismount quickly and fight on the ground, depending on the requirements of the moment.

The first tanks enter Krutojarka, but presently reappear. The company commander gives the radio command. "Krutojarka is being held by the enemy. Clear the town!" The personnel carriers advance past the tanks, which are firing with all their guns, and move toward the edge of the village.

A personnel carrier's tread is hit by a flanking antitank gun. The grenadiers jump out and assault the antitank-gun crew with machine-gun fire, while the driver and the man beside him get out and, under fire, change the broken link of the tread.

The attacking grenadiers have now reached a street at the edge of the village. Startled by the suddenness of the assault, the Russians take cover in houses, bunkers, foxholes, and other hideouts. The grenadiers jump out of the personnel carriers and advance along the street, making good use of grenades, pistols, and bayonets [see cover illustration]. The driver and a second man remain in each carrier.

The personnel carriers skirt around the sides of the village, with the men beside the drivers delivering flanking fire against the buildings. Soon the roofs of the houses are afire. The smoke grows thicker and thicker.

Three tanks push forward along the main street of the village, to support the attack of the grenadiers. We find the smoke an advantage, for it prevents the Russians from discovering that there are relatively few of us. Also, as a result of the poor visibility, the Russians cannot employ their numerous machine guns with full effect. We, for our part, are able to engage in the close-in fighting at which we excel. It is no longer possible to have one command for the company. Officers and noncoms have formed small shock detachments, which advance from street corner to street corner, and from bunker to ditch, eliminating one

Russian nest after another.

A lieutenant holds a grenade until it almost explodes in his hands, and then throws it into a bunker. It explodes in the firing hatch, and enemy soldiers stream out.

The company commander discovers a 37-mm Russian antiaircraft machine gun, and sits down on the saddle. Two men who are with him attack the magazines, which are lying about. Although the commander has never fired this type of cannon before, he succeeds in demoralizing the Russians with its high-explosive projectiles. We take many more prisoners.

When about half the village is in our hands, and when we have captured the Russian commander and his political commissar*, resistance collapses. All prisoners are marched to the rear, and the booty of guns and vehicles is collected. The Panzer Grenadiers advance to the far end of the village, where they climb into the waiting personnel carriers. Most of the tank battalion also has skirted the village, and already has moved further east. Anticipating further action, the Panzer Grenadiers again follow the tanks.

* *Since this account was written, the Russians have discontinued their practice of assigning political commissars to accompany Red Army units.*

GERMAN TACTICS IN THE FINAL PHASES AT KHARKOV

Tactical and Technical Trends,
No. 12, November 19, 1942

In the Russian offensive against Kharkov in May their forces became overextended and were encircled by the Germans. Here they encountered several innovations in the system of hasty fortifications which the Germans threw up to prevent a breakout. These defenses were built around the basic infantry strongpoints, but the way the Germans used their combined arms and armored equipment is revealing.

Figures 1 and 2 in the accompanying sketches outline the systems set up by the Germans around the encircled Russian forces. The sites of the defense areas were selected so that each island of resistance could mutually support the ones adjacent to it.

Each island or center of resistance was formed by three concentric rings. Within the center ring, self-propelled artillery capable of all-around fire was emplaced. In the next outer ring, tanks were camouflaged and embedded in the ground so that they served as pillboxes for their machine guns and other armament. The outer ring was formed by entrenched infantry units provided with their normal infantry weapons, including antitank guns and mortars.

Wire entanglements were laid between the embedded vehicles of the second ring and along the channels of fire of the infantry weapons. Clever signaling devices such as cowbells and self-igniting firecrackers were hung on the wires and nearby bushes to warn of an enemy approach at night.

In the gaps between centers of resistance, minefields were laid and charted, and high-trajectory weapons laid to cover

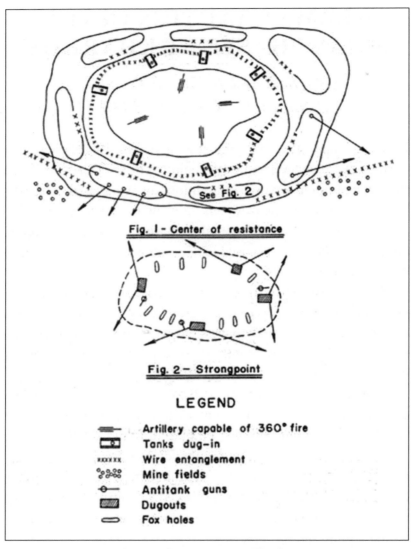

Fig. I - Center of resistance

Fig. 2 - Strongpoint

LEGEND

⟞⟞	Artillery capable of 360° fire
▭	Tanks dug-in
××××	Wire entanglement
°°°°°	Mine fields
⊙—	Antitank guns
▨	Dugouts
⬯	Fox holes

German Strongpoints at Kharkov

defiladed areas.

Outside this system of defensive areas which encircled the Russian troops, mobile combat teams were located, ready to rush to any part of the circumference that might be threatened either from within or without.

More from the same series

Most books from the 'Eastern Front from Primary Sources' series are edited and endorsed by Emmy Award winning film maker and military historian Bob Carruthers, producer of Discovery Channel's Line of Fire and Weapons of War and BBC's Both Sides of the Line. Long experience and strong editorial control gives the military history enthusiast the ability to buy with confidence.

The series advisor is David McWhinnie, producer of the acclaimed Battlefield series for Discovery Channel. David and Bob have co-produced books and films with a wide variety of the UK's leading historians including Professor John Erickson and Dr David Chandler. Where possible the books draw on rare primary sources to give the military enthusiast new insights into a fascinating subject.

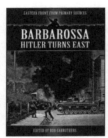
Barbarossa

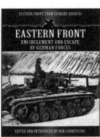
Eastern Front: Encirclement

Götterdämmerung

Eastern Front: Night Combat

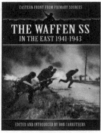
The Waffen SS in the East 1941-1943

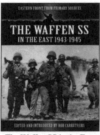
The Waffen SS in the East 1943-1945

The Wehrmacht Experience in Russia

Winter Warfare

The Red Army in Combat

Wehrmacht Combat Reports: The Russian Front

For more information visit www.pen-and-sword.co.uk